L...
with...

When Your Neighbor
Is the Savior

Botrus Mansour

Hope Publishing House
Pasadena, California

Copyright © 2011 Botrus Mansour

For information address:

Hope Publishing House
P.O. Box 60008
Pasadena, CA 91116 - U.S.A.
Tel: (626) 792-6123 / Fax: (626) 792-2121
HopePublishingHouse@gmail.com
www.hope-pub.com

Book Editor: Faith Annette Sand
Cover design: Michael McClary/The Workshop
Front cover picture of Nazareth Village: Tony Bathich

Library of Congress Cataloging-in-Publication Data

Mansour, Botrus.
  When Your Neighbor Is The Savior / Botrus Mansour. - 1st ed.
       p. cm.
  ISBN 978-1-932717-23-5 (alk. Paper)
  1. Mansour, Botrus. 2. Palestinian Arabs--Israel--Nazareth--Biography.
  3. Christians--Israel--Nazareth--Biography.
  4. Arab-Israeli conflict--1993--Influence.
  5. Israel--Ethnic relations.
  6. Palestinian Arabs--Israel--Public opinion.
  7. Public opinion--Israel. I. Title.
  DS113.7.M28 2011
  956.94'5-dc22
  [B]
                    2010046320

Table of Contents

Acknowledgments
Special thanks to a large number of friends who helped
by reading the manuscript and giving comments
and suggestions through the process:
May Arthur, Rev. Philip Hill, Fareed Shehadeh,
Dr. Yohanna Katanacho, Dauod Kuttab, Mark Cutshall,
Samar Mansour Samawi, Bader Mansour,
Dr. Salim Munayer and Cary Summers.

To A'bir,
my companion, best friend and love

1

War Comes Our Way

It was the summer of 2006. I had been in my new job as general director of Nazareth Baptist School for a year. School days tend to be tense and pressured, for it is a continual challenge to keep a thousand students studying, getting a proper education, living at peace with one another and arriving home after school safely. At times it seems more like a churning factory or an intense ant house than a place of calm and studious learning.

Summer time however brings calm and leisure. Only a few staff members wander in and out of the schoolyard where memories have faded of the turmoil at end of term with its elaborate graduation ceremony on the heels of year-end exams. By the time July's heat has descended, everyone has pretty much shifted into low gear. Most of the school staff and administration have scattered for the summer to rest, rev up their engines and prepare for a new academic year while most of the children are off in camps or on vacations.

Unfortunately the tranquil summer schedule of 2006 was shattered when Israel launched a war on Lebanon in retaliation for the kidnapping of two Israeli soldiers by the Shiite militant group, the Hezbollah. Israel began conducting concentrated air raids on Lebanon and in return the Hezbollah began shooting missiles over the entire northern region of our land.

Nazareth, lying in the center of a narrow strip of territory belonging to Israel in the lower Galilee, is about 40 miles from the

Lebanese border—and well within the range of the Hezbollah missiles.

The Israeli Army forces advised the local citizens to stay in "protected surroundings"—which they described as an indoor space away from any external wall of the building. This seemed a lot simpler than what we had been through in 1991 in the first Gulf War. Then there were shelters to go to and gas masks issued with a much more organized and sophisticated defense mechanism put in place.

I was still practicing law part-time the summer of the Lebanese war and one July afternoon as I was working in my office beneath our home in Yaffa of Nazareth (a village just west of the city) trying to catch up on law cases that had piled up because of my new responsibilities at school. Suddenly while at my desk I heard a loud explosion. Even though we tend to be used to sounds of loud bangs—sometimes from airplanes breaking the sound barrier overhead or from exuberant wedding celebrants shooting firecrackers or even guns—this explosion was different. It was accompanied by a high-pitched noise whose source seemed uncomfortably close by.

I jumped up and ran to our home where I found my wife and children in our living room near the television. They were not panicked, but they were bewildered by the strange sound and wondered what it could mean.

We turned on a radio but could find no special news alert, either in Hebrew or in Arabic. A quick search on my computer brought up a popular Hebrew news web site which indicated a missile had fallen in an open area between Nazareth and Yaffa of Nazareth, with no causalities or any damage to property.

The war had started a couple of weeks earlier, and it had been our understanding then that Nazareth would not be targeted. After all, Nazareth is an Arab city with a Muslim majority, so it should have been safe to assume Hezbollah fighters would avoid throwing missiles at us. This turned out to be mere wishful thinking—mainly because their primitive missiles were wildly inaccurate in hitting their targets and, therefore, any slight deviation could get them off target and within striking distance of Nazareth. In fact, by the end of this war, Nazareth had been hit three times. One strike killed two boys in a neighborhood playground in the northern part of town. The Hezbollah leaders offered an extraordinary apology for the killing saying that it was by mistake.

The third missile was even more frightening for us. My son, 13 at the time, had gone with a friend to the YMCA in a crowded part of town to an area with two hospitals and the site that replicates a "first century Nazareth Village."

We turned on the radio to hear the local report which announced the missile had struck the center of Nazareth, claiming it had landed on a garage specializing in Mazda cars. Fear gripped us for we knew our son was only a few hundred yards away from that garage. We tried calling him but got no answer —which made us even more anxious. Later we managed to contact his friend and learned they were, in fact, safe.

Miraculously no causalities resulted from this explosive landing in the middle of town—one reason being it was a Wednesday when, unlike other days of the week, workers get to go home in the early afternoon. The missile hit at around 3 p.m. and most had left work half an hour earlier. Yet the debris was scattered over the entire neighborhood and days later you could still see the fallout from this explosion lying around. These missile attacks terrorized the whole town as people stayed indoors under a self-imposed curfew.

On Wednesdays our church has a Bible study so that day I consulted with two other elders about how we should proceed. It was unanimous that we hold services as usual since it seemed an even more propitious moment for prayer and we certainly all needed to hear a message of encouragement from Scriptures. It was, after all, our reason to exist. We were in Nazareth for a time like this.

Verses from Romans kept ringing in my mind: *"Who shall separate us from the love of Christ? Shall trouble or hardship or persecution or famine or nakedness or danger or sword? As it is written: 'For your sake we face death all day long"* *(Rm 8:35-36)*. Still, few people showed up that evening for Bible study. Those in attendance had a fervent time of prayer plus encouraging words from the Bible and from one another's experiences.

Before this war had started, we had organized big plans for that summer in our church. A team of young people from a church in San Diego were supposed to arrive in Nazareth to help us with our Summer Vacation Bible School. These young people plowed ahead with their plans to show up despite the disturbing news about the war that erupted. Everyone hoped this would turn out to be a short skirmish and that Nazareth would be distant and safe. Still, some of the American parents were understandably worried about their children being in the crossfire of the hostilities.

A meeting was scheduled for the parents of the American youth with one of their pastors who called me to find out how things were going. I wanted the young people to come, but tried not to mix my desire with an objective assessment of the safety issue plus simultaneously displaying faith in the Lord and God's sovereignty and protection. Still I didn't want to give them false assurances, yet I told the pastor I thought Nazareth was safe and that the Hezbollah would not directly aim missiles on Arab Nazareth.

This call took place a few days before the first missile fell on our town. The dust had barely cleared, when a second missile fell. My American assistant, who lives on a hill overlooking the Mazda garage, watched the huge black smoke rising from the explosion and immediately called me to insist I inform the group from California not to come. With a heavy heart, I telephoned the pastor and suggested we postpone the program for a year—which we did, but those young people on opposite side of the globe were disappointed as they watched their summer plans get cancelled.

Each summer our church holds its annual conference in a resort—something common among the Evangelical churches in Israel. These are designed as a family gathering because people here have adopted the Western way of life which makes them extremely busy during the year. Such conferences, therefore, serve as a combined family holiday and a spiritual renewal program. Although I continue to have doubts that these two differing purposes can be accomplished in such a two- or three-day conference, nevertheless as usual we had reserved a resort in a kibbutz north of Nazareth a few months earlier for our conference that was supposed to be held in early August.

Unfortunately this kibbutz was one of the first spots hit in Israel, so our holiday site was closed. My colleagues and I then decided to make reservation at a resort further south and found space available in a hostel in Haifa on the west coast of the Mediterranean. Shortly after that Haifa was hit with numerous missiles, so again we cancelled. We were not going to give up as this was a special gathering for all families, so we decided to go east. This time we reserved a hotel in Tiberias. Prices were slashed because tourists had stopped coming to Israel so it was easily within our budget.

A few days after making the reservation, on my way home from town, I stopped at the butcher's to pick up some meat. The TV was on, and as I waited for my order, I watched the afternoon news story about emergency troops responding to another missile attack—in Tiberias. I could not restrain my bitter smile. As soon as I entered my car I called one of the fellow elders and opened by saying: "Tiberias? You want to go to Tiberias?" He had already heard the news, too, so we shared a gloomy laugh. Thus the reservation for Tiberias was cancelled as well.

Later on we finally managed to hold the conference in a Messianic believers' resort near Jerusalem—away from the range of the Hezbollah missiles. This was in a forested area looking at the mountains of Jerusalem and it turned out to be a much needed and blessed time for the families of the church, most of whom were traumatized by the events.

While the war went on, we had to stay home—which actually gave me the opportunity to begin writing this summary of what had brought me to this stage and explains why the book begins with the thundering sounds of the fighter jets, continuous headline news, commentators and falling missiles in the background. Added to this was the noise emitted by bored children who grumbled from the restraints put on them by the war. Instead of being in camps, swimming pools and with friends as they had hoped on being liberated from school, they unhappily spent the summer stuck at home—with their parents.

So we all looked for escape mechanisms and I found my response to the Lebanese war writing up these notes—which I later amended, cut and expanded.

2

Nazareth

I was born in the Scottish hospital in Nazareth, Oct. 6, 1965, my parent's first child. My father named me "Botrus" after my grandfather, which is the Arabic version of Peter. The French version is Pierre, the Italian, Pierro, and in Spanish Pedro. My eighth birthday coincided with one of the famous dates in new Arab history, the celebration of the Egyptian army's victory over the Israeli Defense Forces in 1973, which caused thousands of Israeli casualties.

My father Atallah Mansour, a journalist and writer, is originally from the village of Jish (Gush Halav) which lies at the foot of Mount Meroun, the highest mountain in Israel. Jish is several kilometers away from the Lebanese border and the southern Lebanese village of Rimesh is even clearly visible from the hilltop on which the village Jish sits.

My grandfather was a struggling builder and farmer, so my father received his elementary education in Jish before being sent to Lebanon for junior high school. His studies there were interrupted when the war of 1948 shut down the border between the newly established state of Israel and Lebanon. In fact, he had to sneak across the border to get back home to Jish in the newly formed state of Israel. When his mother died shortly afterwards, he was thrown on his own devices to get an education which finally landed him as a respected Arab journalist in an Israeli state.

My father's life has been full of adventure for the past five decades as he pursued a career as a journalist and writer for different newspapers and magazines writing in Hebrew, Arabic and English. The highlight of his career was 33 years as journalist in the prestigious Israeli Hebrew newspaper *Haaretz*. He has also written several books in different languages including English, the most recent being an important 2,000-year history of the Christian presence in the Middle East under the title *Narrow Gate Churches: The Christian Presence in the Holy Land under Muslim and Jewish Rule.*

My mother's father was a police officer in the famous village of Cana of Galilee close to Nazareth. It was here Jesus preformed his first miracle, turning water into wine for a wedding feast. Pastors and priests around the world have read the passage about this wedding in John's gospel (1:1-12) as they perform Christian weddings. My grandfather was a police officer with the British troops who ruled Palestine before 1948 which made him an honored personage in the village.

Also, with the influence of my grandmother who read and wrote—a rare phenomenon at that time—my grandfather made sure his daughters and only son received good educations. As a result, four of them became teachers. Only my oldest aunt didn't get proper education because of medical problems. My mother was the first young woman from Cana to earn a high school diploma. She studied at the Baptist school in Nazareth and graduated with its first class in 1955. Soon she would become a teacher in the same school and many years later I became the general director of this same school which is so integral to our family's history.

My father, a Greek Melkite Catholic, married my mother, from a Greek Orthodox background. My maternal grandfather was very proud of his ethnic heritage and used to say "I am an Orthodox and my God is an Orthodox." When my parents married in 1964 it was rare to cross such religious barriers and theirs was considered a mixed marriage because they came from different Christian denominations.

I respect the liturgical churches my parents' families belong to for they have maintained the Christian faith in the Middle East down through the centuries. Nevertheless I personally find the Evangelical churches better capture the Biblical God-given truths and practice them. Yet I'm deeply grateful that my parents reflected in their lives an example of hard-working parents who inculcated us with Christian values and did all that they could to get us children the best education possible.

My parents met, married and made their home in Nazareth, where I was born. My father certainly made sure we had it easier than what he faced as the son of a poor farmer, trying to get a good education in a period of war and unrest and then get into a profession where he could support his family. In fact, he succeeded spectacularly, for he has been widely regarded as an honest and straightforward person, in a culture where honesty and frankness shock many people who are used to flattering, hypocritical or indirect speech. My father also established a reputation as a trustworthy person of integrity who would never accept free meals or compromise himself in any way that would sabotage his name as a credible journalist.

My mother, dedicated to her children and their education and well-being, worked tirelessly as a teacher in school and at home to give us the best childhood anyone could hope for and both my parents put much emphasis on teaching us their Christian faith and values. Yet they were also open-minded and tolerant towards those from other faiths and nationalities, and because of my father's job as a journalist we were regularly visited by Muslims, Jews and Westerners. All in all, my parents' life-styles as well as their words were a compass that would show us the direction we needed to follow.

Christians in Nazareth pride themselves in the fact that Jesus was their neighbor. The main event associated with the town is the Annunciation, where the angel Gabriel proclaimed to Mary the astonishing news that the time had come for the birth of the Messiah and that she, Mary, a simple Nazarene young woman, had been selected by God to bring this Messiah to the world!

This occurred, of course, nine months prior to Christmas so people call the 25th of March "the feast of Nazareth." Several churches in town have "Annunciation" in their names: the

Annunciation church for the Greek Orthodox or the Annunciation Church for the Roman Catholics, etc. We Evangelicals have not followed this tradition. My office in Nazareth Baptist School is 200 yards away from the Greek Orthodox version of the site of annunciation and half a mile from the Catholics' location of the annunciation.

I like to believe Jesus would have attended our school if it had existed in his time. I am sure his parents would want him there because of its scripturally-based ethos and values. However, he probably would have hung around with the children from the public school nearby who give our students a tough time and bully them. He would have wanted to bring them to repentance. I'm sure he was a charming boy—and loved by all who would have appreciated his sincerity, love and compassion. He must have been the first in class. After all he had unlimited knowledge. Didn't he say to Job: "Where were you when I laid the earth's foundation? Tell me, if you understand" (Job 38:4).

In our daily lives as Christians, inhabitants of Nazareth, living this closely to the sites that witnessed those meaningful events, today often take these ancient monuments for granted. In fact, the geographical proximity to these hallowed places sometimes leads to a self-righteous attitude so people frequently feel they are self-sufficient and need no one to teach them about Jesus. They know him personally—"Isn't he the son of Joseph?"

Yet I sometimes wonder if living in Nazareth has any special significance for me. Nazareth today is practically like any other place on earth. Does the fact that some 2,000 years ago the incarnate God of the universe chose to live here bear any meaning to me today? It could even be of significance to the Lord's plans for all humans.

The nature of Jesus' ministry was spiritual. He down-played the physical nature of relationships, concentrating instead on the spiritual. While on the cross, he said to his mother: "Dear woman, here is your son" indicating John (Jn 19:26) and then to John: "Here is your mother" (v. 27). In other words he asked John to treat Mary as his mother, while she was to treat him as her son to compensate for the loss of Jesus.

One interpretation of this instruction is to point out how Jesus emphasized the spiritual bond and relationship in the family of God between believers over and above the physical and ordinary relationship between a mother and son (Mt 19:29).

While Jesus was busy preaching and healing in a home, his mother and brothers came to fetch him. He was sent a message to come out from the house to meet them. His answer showed his perspective is spiritual for he asked rhetorically who were his mother and his brothers? Then "pointing to his disciples, he said: 'Here are my mother and my brothers. For whoever does the will of my Father in heaven is my brother and sister and mother" (Mt 12:46-50). In one fell swoop Jesus elevates the spiritual relationship above the carnal and physical.

One of the most beautiful dialogues recounted in the New Testament occurs when Jesus meets a woman at high noon near the well of Jacob in Samaria (near the city of Nablus-Shechem today). An immoral woman who had had various lovers, she came to the well in the heat of the day to avoid the gossip and condemning glances of the women of the villages who fetched water in the cool of the morning.

Jesus carefully and tactfully leads this famed "woman of the well" step-by-step to a place where she could look for the real living water that can fulfill the thirst of every living being. There were obviously cultural clues that made it apparent to her that Jesus was a Jew. As a Samaritan—the two nations coëxisted side by side in great enmity—she tried to use this fact to change the subject and distract Jesus from his goal. She explained to Jesus that her ancestors had worshipped on this mountain (she was referring to Eibal, the mountain that was sacred for the Samaritans). She puts that in contrast with what Jews claimed should be the locale for worship—Jerusalem.

Instead of allowing her to move the dialogue to the political-religious-geographical arena, Jesus kept on track for he had a greater mission and perspective which kept him from allowing any argument or person to deter him from his calling. His answer showed his interest in the spiritual, in the condition of the heart and in the heavenly, for he said: "Real worshipers will worship in spirit and truth" (Jn 4:24).

Jesus repeatedly emphasized this interest in the spiritual over the physical, so we who live in Nazareth cannot claim any special status with our Lord today. Jesus also made clear that it all depends on the heart and the commitment and faith in the atoning work on the cross regardless of any earthly status or heritage or neighborhood with the savior. In light of this I do not believe Nazareth has a special standing or a higher seat at the banquet of salvation in the eyes of the Lord. However, it has symbolic meaning as a result of Jesus having lived there.

Christians are raised on the Holy Book. From childhood they are immersed in the stories of the Bible. We read them and know their details. We sweep through the pages and imagine we are joining Abraham in Hebron, Zacharias in Jericho, Jacob in Shechem, Peter at his mother-in-law's house in Capernaum and also Jesus as a boy in the town of Nazareth.

A romantic maxim in Arabic states, "I adore you and I adore the ground you walk on." The sensation behind this saying is familiar to every lover. When a man loves a woman he will find her family (including the most despicable members) adorable. He will find her ugly neighborhood attractive and the route of her daily walk sacred. Suddenly he discovers that her hobbies are actually desires and hobbies that were asleep in his character and are now revived. This is part of the human nature and common with lovers.

It applies also to our love for Jesus. We love all that relates to him and naturally also the specific land where he lived will have a special place in our hearts. This is why we love Nazareth and Jerusalem—even with its different features today, 2,000 years after the days the sweet feet of Jesus walked on earth.

An extreme (and even pathological) manifestation of this is the "Jerusalem syndrome" which sometimes occurs when Christians come to Jerusalem and display an extreme pathological disorder. The past magnificent history of the city and the expectation for some kind of breathtaking event of history or of a spiritual or mystical experience has an effect on the visitor. Some even start hallucinating or merging psychologically with a Biblical character. There were several such people suffering from the "Jerusalem syndrome" wandering around in the old city of Jerusalem at the time I lived there. Some claimed and acted as if they were Jesus. These had long beards, sandals on their feet and wore clothes that resembled the first century dress. Others claimed they were David or Elijah.

This love for the places where significant incidents from our history of faith occurred can lead to clashes. The most famous is that of the Jews wanting exclusive control of the Temple Mount in Jerusalem while Muslims on the other hand want to control the Dome of the Rock (which, unfortunately, is actually the same location of the Temple Mount) and its surroundings because according to their belief their prophet Muhammad ascended to heaven on a horse from that spot.

The fact that Nazareth is a center for hundreds of thousands of pilgrims who annually visit to walk in Christ's footsteps and experience a spiritual renewal, has its significance too, for Nazareth has become a place where you can reach out to these multitudes of people from different backgrounds.

Christians have lived in the Holy Land ever since the time of Christ. The continued emigration of Christians away from the Holy Land now in the face of the current Jewish and Muslim majority and hegemony is threatening to leave these Biblical sites having no followers of Christ living around them—as has happened in Turkey with sites such as Ephesus.

Declining numbers of Christian believers in Nazareth, Jerusalem and Bethlehem has significance for the whole of Christendom, not because of some special spiritual importance, but because traditionally they have been a strong symbol and signal in the place where Jesus grew up. If one day all Christians move away from the Holy Land, it will be a negative symbol for Christianity and its more than two billion adherents. Despite the spiritual sphere that Jesus emphasized and his immortal spiritual messages that we are to take our eyes away from the physical, there is actually an importance in the life of believers in the holy sites of Jesus.

Furthermore, the fact that Jesus was not welcomed in Nazareth and performed just a few miracles there has significance in that we, as Nazarenes today, would want to bring the glory back to the place Jesus chose to live and repudiate what our predecessors did in this spot.

Some faithful believers in Nazareth today try to give Nazareth some deeper mystical meaning, pointing out that Jesus could not perform many miracles here because of a lack of faith in the village. They also note that Jesus was chased out of the synagogue in Nazareth and out of town altogether and claim that Jesus' honor in his hometown of Nazareth must be regained before he can return to the world.

I personally see the need for a revival in Nazareth as in any other place on earth and can anticipate the flavor and beauty of a revival in Nazareth itself of all places. Nevertheless, this rationale of the significance of modern Nazareth due to its past is certainly reflected in my ministry and calling.

"Can anything good come out of Nazareth?" This question pondered by Nathanael 2,000 years ago has created a great deal of speculation, interpretation and a folklore of healthy humor for the people of Nazareth ever since.

When Philip met the son of God face to face, he was enthusiastic. The word "enthusiastic" derives from "in-theo," e.g. "in God." In the case of Philip its original meaning applied. Philip was both excited and in an in-God state of mind. In his enthusiasm he reported to Nathanael that they had "found the one Moses wrote about in the Law, and about whom the prophets also wrote—Jesus of Nazareth, the son of Joseph" (Jn 1:45). Nathanael, a cynical, down-to-earth person who was a reluctant believer, expressed his doubts about Philip's revelation and asked: *"Nazareth! Can anything good come from there?"* (v. 46).

How does a person who had met the glorious Jesus face a cynical attitude that clearly extinguishes the spirit? Philip was in no mood to argue with Nathanael. He just uttered three words that constitute practical advice, halting by it an argument over the possibility that a wretched village with a bad reputation could be the hometown of the messiah. Those three famous words ring down through the centuries: "Come and see!"

Little did Philip imagine that his simple question would become the center of folklore about the nature of the people of Nazareth. He merely asked Nathanael to come and experience for himself instead of relying on stereotypes and prejudices he had against the bad-reputed village. He might have thought it a useless argument and agreed with Nathanael's negative attitude towards this small village known more for its robbers and criminal element than for anything else.

Fuad Sakhnini, pastor of the Evangelical Baptist church in Nazareth for the last half century, used to say it is true that nothing good comes out of Nazareth, rather, it stays in it! My brother and I decided to create a web site to raise the awareness of the Christian West on what is happening in this area of the world. As this was going to be a Christian web site from Nazareth, we decided to look for an interesting and appealing name. After considering several names like "Jesus' neighbors" or "15 minutes from Armageddon" or "view of Armageddon" plus more conventional names like "news from Nazareth," in the end we decided to call it "come and see" and obtained the address www.comeandsee.co.il and started posting both stories from other web sites about the region as well as original articles. Later on we added the domain www.comeandsee.com. "Nazareth Village," a museum theme park of Nazareth from the first century used the same slogan as well.

3

Exile from Nazareth

When I was two, the Six Day War broke out. My parents recount how I stood on our balcony in the Nazareth neighborhood where we lived singing children's songs about airplanes as the Israeli fighter jets passed over our home on their way to bomb the Golan Heights. This war forever changed the peoples of the Middle East.

My life was affected soon after, for after the war we moved from Nazareth to Jerusalem. Later we came back to Nazareth, so I always consider myself a Nazarene and feel it is a great honor to be like Jesus Christ, a native of this hilly town in Galilee.

After the occupation of East Jerusalem and the West Bank by Israel in 1967, my father was asked by his newspaper *Haaretz* to move from Nazareth to Jerusalem to cover the newly occupied territory of East Jerusalem and the West Bank. As an Arab with a mastery of Arabic, he was prepared to report on what was happening in that area. He could talk to local residents and leaders of the area and present a more accurate and better picture for the Israeli reader. My mother resigned from the Baptist School so we could go to Jerusalem.

We moved to a rented flat in East Jerusalem's Wadi Eljouse neighborhood where we lived peaceably side by side with our Palestinian Muslim neighbors for four years. During this sojourn, the family expanded and a new brother and sister were added. My father acknowledges that this period of time was both exciting and stormy professionally because of all that was happening in Jerusalem and the West Bank after the occupation of Israel. On the other hand, we all treasured the experience of living with our friendly neighbors in the family-like atmosphere of the East Jerusalem Arabs—with whom we have maintained contact ever since those days just after the Six-Day War.

I began kindergarten in Jerusalem in schools run by various Catholic monasteries, while my mother taught in an Arab neighborhood of Jerusalem. A neighbor, originally from Turkey but married to a Palestinian, babysat for my brother, whom she still calls "my son." These were special days.

Years later I returned to Jerusalem to study at the Hebrew University. Their main campus, where humanities, social sciences and law are taught, is located on Mount Scopus—a five-minute walk from where our home was in Wadi Eljouse. There will always be a special, warm place in my heart for Jerusalem —a fantastic city where every stone carries thousands of years of history.

The Lord provided me with a unique experience that other children in Nazareth rarely get in a new environment that was transformative. After four years of living in Jerusalem, with intense day and night work covering the news in this embroiled region, my father received a scholarship from the British Council to continue his studies at Ruskin College in Oxford, England. The paper granted him a two-year sabbatical, and suddenly our family of five flew to England for a new adventure.

The first year we lived in a nearby village called Eynsham, a suburb of Oxford. The second year we moved to a duplex complex for international students' families who come to Oxford for education from the various colleges around the city. The daily acclimatization in the duplex with Nigerian, Australian, Syrian and Indian children was a great experience for me.

The two years we were in England, I went to English schools. In Eynsham I attended an experimental school that taught using new educational methods. This school had a swimming pool where I had my first swimming lessons. I also vaguely remember our teacher asking us to trap an insect in the school fields to bring back to the laboratory to examine it and observe under the microscope. We were expected to report to the teacher about the movement of the insect. As someone involved today in education, the fact that this advanced research approach took place in the first grade, 37 years ago, is amazing. I am still astonished at the progress and development in the English educational system even in the early 70s of last century.

The second year in England I was sent to a Christian private school (St. Philips and St. James) in Oxford. I recall not having to carry a bag to school for all the extra activities took place in the school in the long study day that ended at four in the afternoon. Because I was not studying Arabic at school, my mother taught me Arabic, my native tongue, in the late afternoon while the other youngsters in the complex played on the lawn or in a special recreation room available to us.

Learning Arabic was a daily torture and I could not comprehend why my mother wanted to teach me this strange lan- guage—Arabic—while my thoughts (and ears) followed the others who got to play in the playground outside our flat. Nevertheless and despite the perceived torture at the time, the classical Arabic language I learned from my mother was of a great help to me later when I returned to my homeland and went straight to the third grade.

At the Oxford school we were given a hot lunch daily. How well I remember the long break after the meal. The learning method there was honed to the progress of each individual student. So we were assigned books to read according to our level of improvement. I remember little else about their pedagogy, but I do recall playing colonial games with the Brits and when it came to "Cowboys and Indians" I instantly was assigned to the Indian group because of my dark skin color. Ever since then I've been proud of my affiliations with the minority and oppressed groups around me.

The Lord blessed me with this privilege of studying in an advanced educational British system within a multi-cultural environment. After these two years I spoke English fluently, even though when we arrived back in Israel I had almost forgotten my Arabic. Still, with English as the language of the modern world, mastering spoken English at that early age turned out to be a boon.

This cross cultural experience would also prove to be helpful in what the Lord was preparing me for the future.

4

Back to Nazareth

After the two school years ended in England, we left behind amazing Oxford, packed our belongings into a container to be shipped back to Israel, and then our family of five jumped into a new 1973 Ford Escort station wagon for an even further adventure—driving our way back to our beloved homeland.

The trip was phenomenal. We ferried the car to Holland where we stayed for four days with my parents' friends. Then we drove on to Germany and Switzerland where we stayed with more friends. Continuing on to Venice, my father drove while my mother navigated with a map in hand. My brother, sister and I slept, played and had a few fights in the back seat. Ever since that trip I have liked station wagons. Of course, today with the European Union and the breakthrough of national borders, such a trip is not as momentous as it was in 1973.

In Venice we boarded a ship to cross the Mediterranean, with a stop in Athens, arriving in Haifa several days later. Never will I forget our ship sliding slowly to its berth on the shores of Israel early one June morning. The beauty of the city of Haifa at the foot of Mount Carmel is forever engraved in my memory. The fog slowly lifted as our ship approached the shore revealing Mt. Carmel, where Elijah the prophet encountered the prophets of Baal.

In those days trips abroad were still rare, and much more so when it was a return after a two-year absence, so a large contingent of our extended family awaited us at the Haifa port. Soon I was being introduced to a cousin just a few months older than me. They explained she would guide me around the public library in the Nazareth market after they had registered me there. After the tears and all the welcoming hugs and kisses, we were soon in a car convoy headed back to Nazareth.

Thus England earned a special place in my heart after these two years. The English I learned there gave me an advantage over my peers in Nazareth, which, in fact, became a two-edged sword. On the one hand I was not interested in learning the rules of grammar because I spoke and wrote English intuitively and was able to identify mistakes by listening. This turned out to be a problem in writing English in the upper schools because I had neglected grammar basics in school feeling I had no need for them.

Living far from Israel was a refreshing experience for the whole family, but it was clear to me, even at that early age that I would always prefer living in Nazareth. When we returned to my birthplace—beloved Nazareth—my father naturally chose to enroll me in the Nazareth Baptist School where my mother had graduated and later taught. Of course, I'm not overly objective when I claim it was then and is still the best school in town— and one of the best in the whole country.

The interview between my father and the principal and his deputy was memorable. He tried to convince them to accept me into the third grade, while the principal explained that since 42 students in the second grade were being promoted to third grade in a number of weeks there was no room for me. My father is persuasive. He rejoindered with an easy solution: "We will add one more chair and desk to the crowded class and Botrus can then join." He was unwilling to accept a "no" for an answer.

In the end, the principal and his deputy principal gave up and the latter said that if I would cut my long hair to the standard the school regulations required, they would fit me in. This was their way of admitting me to the third grade. The deputy was Fuad Haddad who became my English and history teacher, then principle and general director of the school and is now chair of the school board. Today, 37 years later, "Ostaz" [teacher in Arabic] Fuad is a close friend and we work together as a team. Down through the years he has proven to be the sweetest and most humble Christian you could meet. He is Mr. "Nazareth Baptist School" where he has been faithfully serving in different functions for more than 50 years.

Soon after our return to Israel, the 1973 war erupted and my dad left to carry out his journalism assignment on the Golan Heights—one of the battlefields. The ensuing years continued to bring excitement our way. We were living in an apartment my father had purchased when he was single. It later accommodated our small family of three before the 1967 war, but now we were five and the neighborhood that had been built as apartments for singles and small families became a lively, crowded and packed neighborhood.

It was a nightmare for my parents, but a paradise for us, the youngsters. The complex of four small apartments where we lived had nine other children our ages plus dozens of children in the neighborhood. Daily we played "hide and seek," "the seven stones" (a distorted version of baseball played in a small area), or various other pickup games. In addition, the neighborhood is adjacent to a vacant hillside where we spent hours playing soccer and various games or built go-carts out of wires intended for fences or lit fires, climbed trees, or generally kept ourselves entertained with the rest of the kids from our neighborhood.

Yet I was the only one around who attended the Nazareth Baptist School—which was relatively far from where we lived— and my parents had difficulty in getting me to study and do my homework. The other children didn't seem to have any and it was a struggle to keep me from pursuing fun to meet school obligations. I played "hide and seek" with the friends in the neighborhood and "hide and seek" from my parents.

At the bottom of our neighborhood hill there was a valley on the side of which is the land where "Nazareth Village" is located today. Never did I imagine that here, some 25 years later, I would be part of a group establishing this replica of a first-century village which currently attracts tens of thousands of visitors each year. Who would have imagined at the time that our playground where we avidly played soccer—my main hobby in those days—would one day become a source of Biblical insight and a spiritual experience for many.

My parents knew the life-style we were living was not conducive for raising their three children. As soon I got to high school I would need privacy, quiet and a place to study. Moving to a larger home was inevitable, so they succeeded in finding a larger house in the nearby Yaffa of Nazareth where we moved when I was in my teens and my obsession with soccer was abating.

High school days were replete with typical teenager angst, mostly involving "love," "charm" and "crushes." In those good, old conservative days most of the fellows waited impatiently for chances to pursue their latest "sweetheart" but we rarely had much success.

But this was the time that I was introduced to another kind of love—eternal love.

In the mid-70s when I was a twelve-year old sixth grader, I was obsessed with soccer. I studied the sports sections in the Hebrew morning newspapers my father brought home in addition to the Arabic paper that was delivered. I was known among my classmates as the expert on what was happening in soccer teams in Israel and abroad. I played soccer in school and in the neighborhood playground whenever I had a chance.

I was a right-wing attacker and my dream was to play in the official league for the town's leading team: Hapoael Nazareth—which was also the best Arab team in Israel at the time. Young men from our neighborhood played on the team. My dream was to score a goal for the team, to run towards the cheering crowd and jump on the fence that separated the playing ground from the fans. Nazareth soccer fans were very enthusiastic and the fence was dangerously close to the playground. In my dreams I could see the adoring fans surround me with love and adoration and chant my name.

Our Christian education teacher at Nazareth Baptist School, George Laty, was a character, but with an overwhelming capacity to love people in general and students in particular. Compassion poured from him. He was kind and considerate. The impact he had during the years on students was immense. Today more than 18 years after his death, he is remembered among the hundreds of graduates that he taught as someone who was made in Christ's image. He was also generous beyond measure, giving from his own savings to needy families.

At Christmas he would tell the story of the missionary to China, Lootie Moon, and even began a charity campaign called the "Lottie Moon campaign" to help the poor, collecting contributions and encouraging students from the school to give and assist needy families with the funds collected. He wanted to spread the festive atmosphere of Christmas to these families as well. Soon people identified the Lottie Moon campaign as the "Laty Moon offering," after his own name.

We were fascinated with the story of George Laty's conversion. Before knowing Jesus personally, he was a Communist atheist. During the 1948 war he was brought to trial in a military court because the army found a photo of him in military uniform with a rifle and declared him to be a "terrorist." He was about to be executed when the Lord rescued him from certain death. Later he was rescued from death miraculously two other times.

One day in 1976 George Laty, who taught Bible in our school, announced that there would be revival meetings in the nearby Baptist church that week. Knowing our love of playing football and to encourage us to attend the meetings, he said we could play football in the school yard nearby before the service. That appealed to us, so along with two friends, we accepted the invitation and came to play football.

Faster than we could imagine, our play time was over and the revival meetings were about to start. We had no choice but to keep our promise, so we three sweaty boys went into the church to see what the big fuss was all about. It was not the first time I had entered the church since we held our chapel services there, but on entering this day it appeared more polished and seemed brighter than usual.

We sat on the bench in the back row—but we were hard to miss in the midst of the men and women who filled the church.

The singing was entertaining as it was led by our beloved teacher George who had an enthusiastic and theatrical manner. Afterwards, an American guest preacher gave a sermon which was interpreted into Arabic. Suddenly in the middle of the sermon, this tall American preacher took a green dollar bill from his pocket, raised it high, and said, "Will one of the three young lads sitting on the back bench please come here and take this dollar?" The congregation turned en masse and looked at us in amusement. We were embarrassed and looked at one another wondering: What's the catch? What do these people want from us? Where's the trap?

Living in the Holy Land you learn early in life there's nothing free, so there had to be a trick. After several long moments, one of my two friends shrugged and lurched forward to the pulpit, stretching out his hand to take the dollar bill, but the preacher snatched it away saying: "Just a minute! Let me ask you a question: Did you work for the money? Why do you think you should take it?"

My friend blushed, waited for a second and grumbled and said in Arabic: "Balash!" [a loose translation renders this as "no need, don't worry"] hurrying back to his seat in the midst of the crowd's laughter. But the preacher urged him to return, and with the encouragement of some of the church members, my friend returned, whereupon the preacher came down from the pulpit and gave the dollar to my happy friend.

The preacher then went on to relate this undeserved dollar to the grace of God manifested in salvation through Jesus Christ. My buddy did nothing to earn the dollar just as we did nothing to earn personal salvation. All we had to do was accept it just as my friend had accepted the dollar (albeit with some reluctance). The lesson was well received and illustrated nicely.

At the end of the sermon, the preacher extended an invitation to accept the real thing. The worth of such grace is not a dollar note, nor a million dollars or even a billion dollars: it was priceless. The salvation of Christ for those of us who believe is always free!

The prophet Isaiah captured this thought in the words: "Hey, all who are thirsty, come to the water! You who have no money, come! Buy and eat! Come! Buy wine and milk without money and without cost!" (55:1). It did not take us long to decide. We went forward and prayed with the preacher surrendering our lives and trust in Jesus as Lord and Savior.

Going home that night I committed myself sincerely to Christ pledging that from then on I would be a good boy and behave myself. This was the extent of my understanding of what salvation meant. Like Saul who went to fetch his father's donkeys but found the kingdom, I went to play soccer but found salvation. I was very young and my pledge to behave myself lasted only a few days, but another three years would pass before I had a real encounter with Jesus Christ.

If it was soccer that brought me to church the first time, it was wrestling that attracted me the second time. I never loved wrestling but the attraction was appealing even for me.

In April 1979 we were told a Lebanese preacher, who previously had been a famous wrestler, was coming to the Baptist church's revival meetings. It was rumored this giant of a man habitually broke pulpits in the zeal of his preaching. Who would want to miss such an attraction?

Morris Jeries was a not a typical giant. He was six feet tall but we could see his muscles rippling under the sleeves of his jacket. When he took a deep breath, we could see the fine figure of this godly man. He began his sermons asking the audience to focus on the sermon and not to leave while he was preaching since this was a distraction for the others there. When anyone disregarded this request intentionally (and brave people who would want to anger this mighty wrestler were few) or unintentionally, he would stop preaching and stare at the guilty party. No one wanted to be in the shoes of the "guilty" person.

He started his sermons speaking softly, almost in a whisper. Then slowly his voice would rise and if you were lucky you would witness one of his roars accompanied by the scene of his mighty fist being raised and the striking down on the pulpit, smashing it beyond repair. It was not only his image and style that made Pastor Morris famous but the content. He spoke about the unexpected death of all human beings and about the wrath of God on those who do not accept his love and mercy in Jesus.

In Arab culture, people do not talk directly about illnesses or about death. People still refer to cancer as "that illness" or even use the English word "cancer" and not the Arabic. Arabs also smooth references to death with obscure phrases like "after a long life," or "when God returns back his deposit," etc.

Pastor Morris, however, was blunt and spoke openly about these issues in a way that made his listeners have to face the reality of life, illness and death. He had numerous heart-breaking stories of people who were struck by lorries after leaving meetings and not accepting the message of salvation, or children who did not accept Christ but were killed and broke the hearts of their parents. After one such sermon in the spring of 1979 I trembled with fear and came forward to surrender my life to Jesus, praying and asking for forgiveness of my sins. Later I understood that practically my first decision to accept Jesus as Lord and Savior brought me into the kingdom, but this new commitment brought me to a new awareness.

During his days on this planet, Jesus had different ways of attracting people to his message. Some were healed and then believed and followed. To others he revealed deep spiritual secrets and they, too, followed him. To others he revealed himself in a vision. So it is today, for each person's experience encountering Christ is unique, even though some give different names to an essentially similar experience.

I appreciate hearing from others how they came to their Christian faith; however, I believe that in the eyes of the Lord there is no gradation to the born-again experience, even if some do talk about that. Like most Christians I know, I had my ups and downs, my times of fervent spiritual growth with Jesus and other times when I slid away; however I always felt that from that evening, I was born again to be a new person in Christ Jesus.

A group of my classmates came to know the Lord at the same revival meetings of Morris Jeries and so we decided to form a group of a dozen or so students who would come to church each Sunday and demand having a Sunday school class of our own. We are greatly indebted to those who sacrificed their time and came especially to teach us Sunday school. Today I can appreciate the need for dedicated people who would give their lives for the youth. The impact through them on the new, young believers lasts a lifetime. In my position today as elder in the church and general director of the school I do my best to promote such programs, for it certainly made a difference in my life and I wish to be instrumental in having the same effect on the lives of precious youngsters today.

I wish I could say my field of study was chosen after prayer and fasting and asking the guidance of the Lord. It wasn't. Nevertheless I believe the Lord guided my footsteps and put in my heart the desires for pursuing a law degree.

I always liked and did well in mathematics, but I also liked languages, especially reading comprehension and composition— but not grammar. Still I could not decide what professional field I should pursue. Everybody kept talking about "the promising future" of computer sciences and engineering and my father encouraged me to pursue this field. In order to prepare for this, I enrolled in an extracurricular course in the High Technology Institute of Israel (the prestigious Technion) when I was still in the tenth grade. I took a course in PLC, which was then an important computer language but which today has become extinct.

But during my eleventh grade, a revolution in my head started that concerned my future career. During a "student day" our class was to put on a play that took place in a court room. I played the part of one of the lawyers. I can't even remember the subject of the play, yet I still recall the joy the opportunity gave me to present my explanations and pleas. It was exciting to be involved in a heated argument. The compliments I received after the play didn't hurt!

But then, I was full of joy during composition classes. In high school we were blessed with an Arabic teacher who required us to write compositions on different subjects which he then asked us to read aloud in class and lead a discussion about the topic. This added experience convinced me that law was the field I should pursue. I liked to reason, write, talk and defend the weak. I graduated from high school with a physics-mathematics major and an average that enabled me to study the subject that I wanted—law. My dad was not disappointed as later on my brother pursued a degree in software engineering.

The graduation ceremony from school was touching. Rev. Dr. Dale Thorne, an American missionary who served as the general director of the school for 17 years, handed me the certificate. It was his last year as general director before moving on. Two decades later he would join in our efforts to promote the school and head the nonprofit organization we established in the U.S.

I finished high school with feelings of joy mixed with sadness. We had completed an important stage in life but it required leaving a beloved school and classmates that were closer than brothers. I thought that my only relationship with the school in the future would be as a parent when I would send my children to study there.

The Lord had different plans.

5

University, Work and Marriage

I went to the Hebrew University in Jerusalem in order to study law, but my studies did not go smoothly. Besides law, I took economics for a short term at the Haifa University and computer science at the Technion in Haifa. During my years in Jerusalem I was exposed to all the variations of university life. The faculty of law in Jerusalem is the best in the country, together with the Tel-Aviv University. Its graduates include key political luminaries such as ex-Prime Minister Ehud Olmert and many high court judges—of which some return to teach at the university. In the faculty I was exposed to the Israeli Ashkenazi (Jews originally from Europe) and the elite establishment of the Israeli legal system.

But living in Jerusalem also exposed me to the social and political life on Mt. Scopus. This campus included many Arab students—the cream of the crop from the cities and villages of Galilee and the triangle with Jewish students and foreigners. Life on campus was stimulating and shaped our characters. This was also my first experience away from my parents. The expectations to study and succeed were great but the attractions of exploring our freedom as young students on campus were equally compelling. The tensions between these two magnets accompanied students all the way through their days there.

The campus in Jerusalem was immersed in political activities, all kinds of romantic relationships, gossip, burnishing, foppishness, cards, games, parties, and more. Among the student body were the studious and square hard workers who studied endlessly, eyes red from studying all night long. Their efforts paid off and were evident during the exam time when their rooms in the students' complex became pilgrimage centers for many of their colleagues who came to get their notes to photocopy or to get help preparing for scary exams.

On the other hand were those of the leisure class who sat on the lawn tanning themselves in the cold sun of Jerusalem. During term time they ignored the studious ones who faithfully attended lectures rooms, sought out help from the lecturers and spent hours in the library. The "lawn specialists" spent endless hours in one of the scattered cafeterias, discoursing endlessly with their critics and observers who had an opinion about everything on earth. They attended every party and social event, set up card tables in their dorms to play endlessly and could be found in the cinema halls on campus or any place that looked like entertainment.

It's been a long time since those days have passed, but I must admit I was not part of the studious group of students.

As Arab students at the university we did not feel comfortable in the Western (Jewish-Israeli) part of Jerusalem. We regarded this as the fanatic area where many religious ultra-orthodox Jews and Arabs-haters dwelt. Everywhere you went there it was filled with soldiers and security checks that added to your feelings of alienation towards the western side of town.

Yet, I was introduced, like many of my colleagues in the 80s, to the Palestinian population of East Jerusalem. Mount Scopus is actually located on the east side of Jerusalem among different Arab neighborhoods. The old market located inside the famous walls of ancient Jerusalem is a 15-minute walk from the university dorms. Visits to the old market (the *souq,* in Arabic) were common and refreshing. There you could find good humus (a chickpea dish), restaurants, cinema theaters, bakeries for hot bread and special shops for other Middle Eastern sweets. You could also visit significant sites like the Church of the Holy Sepulcher (site of Jesus' tomb), the Mount of Olives, Gethsemane, as well as the Garden Tomb for meditation and prayer.

With my exposure to the campus life and being away from my roots in Nazareth with our Baptist church and my home, I began to drift away from the Lord and started to doubt my beliefs. I became active in a student cell of a rising political party and started smoking, too. Various friends from the Christian Student Fellowship did not give up on me and persisted in encouraging me to join their Bible studies. Finally I surrendered my life afresh to the Lord and am glad to say I'm still walking with Christ today.

Soon I became deeply involved in the Christian Student Fellowship. We had Bible study meetings off campus and students from three different universities convened there weekly for Bible study, fellowship and singing. We had special parties for Christmas and Easter and became involved with the local Evangelical churches of Jerusalem, Bethlehem and Ramallah.

Our meetings were flourishing, lives were touched and people from Christian backgrounds who had never known the Lord began attending regularly and asking to know more. I was once told that before I came to Jerusalem to study, the students' group had a faithful nucleus of four students who met weekly for a year to pray, study Scriptures and plead with the Lord to bring revival to their meetings. The Lord answered their prayers in the year that followed and I was witness to the spiritual renewal. Abir, who would become my wife, was part of that small group of four.

Messianic Jewish students and foreigners also met in Jerusalem and we occasionally had joint meetings for both groups. This mixture of Christian Israeli Arabs from Galilee, Messianic Jews, Arab Christian Palestinians from the West Bank as well as Koreans, Americans, Finnish, British and other nationalities coming together to worship the Lord was fascinating. Despite differences in language and culture all were united in the love of the Lord.

I went on to become involved with the student fellowship at the national level and was elected chair of the board of students. To this day this body of Christian students continues the ministry of serving the Messiah in the land as Arabs, Jews and ex-patriots worship together.

As someone blessed by this ministry, I can appreciate its importance. Campus life for a young person away from church and family can be very tempting. The pressures of study and the struggles of relationships as well as the political and atheistic agenda of those around was very heavy, so the fellowship of Christian students provided a counter-force in difficult and dark times.

Jerusalem was not only a blessing because of the renewed commitment I made to the Lord and the finishing of my studies, but also because there I met my dear future wife. I returned from Jerusalem with a double fortune: a wife and a degree. Abir, a sweet young woman from Kuffur Yassif near Acre, came to Jerusalem to study psychology and English. She had been raised in the local Evangelical church in her village and we met at the Christian students group. She was not only dedicated to the Lord, but she was (and still is) good-looking, bright, gentle and loving.

In due time and after prayer for guidance, I proposed to her in March 1989. She accepted. It was euphoric. As an engaged couple we had a wonderful time touring Jerusalem and dreaming about the future. Later in July 1992 we got married.

The Lord has blessed me with this wonderful godly person to be at my side. Without her support, encouragement and backup I would have never accomplished what I have so far. She also is a wonderful mother and loved by many—and no one doubts she is my better half. While I am task-oriented and tough at times, she brings gentleness and tenderness.

During my study in Jerusalem, I worked for a law office that represented Palestinians before the Israeli authorities. This experience colored the Jerusalem experience sharply. I felt what was not known to many Israelis—the Palestinians were crushed and oppressed. It was inevitable that I sympathize with them.

When I finished my law degree in 1992 I returned to Nazareth as an apprentice in the district court. There in chambers was a Jewish judge who turned out to be a real character. Fluent in Arabic, he also had an amazing sense of humor. Although he was a brilliant jurist, these were his last days before retiring and he was no longer keen to do hard work and write rulings but preferred that each side settle. When the two factions would bargain in his chambers in order to reach a financial settlement, he would humorously hold his wallet and offer to personally pay the difference between them in order to finalize the compromise and reach a settlement.

Later on in my apprenticeship I moved to an office specializing in torts (mainly compensation for physical damage) in Haifa. There I dealt with a much saner population than inhabited Jerusalem with its fanatics and hostilities. In comparison Haifa was a normal, quiet Westernized city.

In October 1993, I passed the law bar exams and our first-born son was born the next month. We gave him my father's name "Atallah" as is the custom in our society, and it means: God's gift—a name similar to Jonathan, Nathanael and Matthew.

On the day Atallah was born I happened to be in Haifa with my lawyer-boss at a Christian home for retarded children. He wanted to investigate if any of these children were there due to medical negligence (in birth or afterwards) so he could sue for compensation. For me it was a horrifying and depressing experience to see these gentle, pure creatures captured in distorted and paralyzed bodies. Returning home from work I found that Abir was on her way to the hospital to deliver. With the scenes from the morning still haunting me, my heart was filled with praise to God the minute my healthy, beautiful son was born.

A great joy filled my soul that day and my prayer is that this great love will not cause me to hinder his steps in the future, but rather that I can become a spring board for him to fulfill what the Lord wants for his life. Being a father helped me grasp the meaning of the special relationship of father and son—and gave me a glimpse of how the Lord deals with us. When we ache, God aches. When my son hurts his nail, I identify with his pain too.

Like any parents, our raising Atallah was a mixture of joy and anxiety. He was our first born and the first grandson to both our parents. We wanted to do everything according to the book. Today he is finishing high school and remains a joy both to me and his mother.

I worked in Haifa for over a year, first as an intern and then as a lawyer. In November 1996 when our second child was born we called her Lamma. The joy was great but naturally we were less tense. Girls in a home add tenderness and gentleness. Lamma added that as did our third and last child Mai born in May 2003. God has been good to us giving us three healthy children. God has also given us grace and strength to raise them in the fear and admonition of the Lord. It remains a day-to-day job we still find challenging and our hope is to do it according to God's will.

After my time in Haifa, I moved to a law firm in Nazareth. With my studies and exams behind me, I was in my chosen career, settled down with a wonderful wife and great family. Yet from hindsight I can see the Lord was preparing me for a purpose that began to unfold. When I committed my life to Christ I became a new creation and was born again. This new man now had a new purpose in life—to live for the One who died for our sake and to commit each day to follow and obey this Master, Savior and Redeemer.

All of us who are in Christ have different life-styles, callings, views and relationships. So what was mine? Differences between those who follow Christ are vast: the pious Orthodox woman from Greece, the American Southern Evangelical, the Canadian Mennonite pacifist, the human rights Episcopalian activist, the Mexican Catholic, the Messianic Jewish teacher in Jerusalem or the Arab Evangelical in Nazareth, like myself.

We can conclude that no follower of Christ operates in a vacuum. The new purpose of living will have different manifestations in each follower of Christ. The expectation that we will find an army of believers with the same mind set, views, attitudes, relationships and calling is naïve and misleading.

Our God is a creative God. Observing the vast variety of species in the universe gives us a glimpse of God's love for creativity. Each human is created with a different genome and a totally unique personality. The Lord obviously opted for diversity in nature and therefore we can expect that our fellowship and relationship with God would be equally diverse. The Lord is as pleased with Latino worship styles as with the Japanese seriousness of studying the Bible, or the American enthusiasm as with the Chinese perseverance in face of myriad persecutions.

This diversity is not just on the nationalistic and cultural level between different peoples, but also on the individual level. A theologian friend keeps talking about contextual theology. So the new person in Christ will need to contextualize their calling to the specific setting of their life. The Holy Spirit that gives us this new life in Christ will guide us in our daily life, helping us set our goals and calling—all in the context and relevant to our specific life. Thus 2,000 years ago, the Holy Spirit used the talents and characteristics of each one of the authors of Scripture to write God's Word. Paul's personal attributes as a rabbinate highly educated Jew is evident in his epistles. Luke was a meticulous physician and his detailed style is evident in his gospel. King David was a shepherd and musician and his poetic style is evident in the Psalms.

I know God did not place me in my specific setting by coincidence or whim. God has a purpose for the life of each believer and wants to deal with the circles that compose my life from a new perspective in the light of the birth of the Spirit. The same is true for every Christian. Of course, our personal, nationalistic and cultural heritage will be evident in the new life and calling. The Lord takes all our circles of identification, belonging, culture, nationality, society and gives them new meaning through the new purpose of life and calling of the new creation.

The new creatures in Christ have been called for a mutual ministry—not to work alone or in a vacuum striving to fulfill their own aspirations or dreams, but rather to participate with God in fulfilling God's purpose—which is unique and specially designed by God even before this new creature was born.

Living as an Arab-Israeli-Palestinian-Evangelical Christian in Nazareth, Israel, brings its complications. How was I to fulfill my calling to serve the Lord in the Lord's home town—especially since I was part of a tiny minority with conflicting affiliations in a broiling country? How was I to serve Christ as a living sacrifice (Rm 12:1) when I am part of a minority within a minority within a minority in Israel?

When I am abroad and someone asks where I'm from, I always answer "Israel" which evokes various responses. Some are excited thinking I am a Jew. Then I explain that actually I am an Arab which usually makes them think I am a Muslim, which means I must clarify even further that I am actually a Christian. The assumption then is that I am either Catholic or Orthodox, as are most Christians in Israel, but finally the truth is out: I'm an Evangelical.

So my question has been: What would Jesus want an Arab, Israeli, Palestinian and Christian Evangelical from his hometown to do?

The answer slowly came into focus and I realized the Lord had been shaping and preparing me to minister for him in his own hometown in a most unique role. I had received values from home and later accepted the Lord as my Savior. I had walked the journey of faith for a while and experienced falls and victories. I was well trained and having lived in Oxford, Nazareth and Jerusalem gave me cross-cultural experiences. I was also married with children.

But I felt it was time for a new challenge. What sort of contribution could I make to the church and the wider community? How could I best be of service to the Lord in the specific setting of Nazareth and Galilee? What were the dynamics of this environment? What were the challenges of the community and what could be my part in helping the church reach out to the community in the hometown of Jesus?

On the one hand I needed to know more of my environment. As Karl Barth said, Christians "should have the Bible in one hand and the newspaper in the other." So we needed to be open to learn about our community and culture in order to address the challenges as Christians. If it's not relevant, the Bible is not effective. I believe this is one of the greatest challenges of ministry anywhere: to be relevant.

6

Living Stones after Pentecost

What are the roots of the Arab Christians that I am to minister among? After Christ's resurrection, he promised his disciples he would not leave them as orphans but would send them the Holy Spirit—and this happened on the day of Pentecost in Jerusalem when suddenly the Holy Spirit came down on those who were praying and baptized them with an evangelical fervor that took this message to the ends of the known world.

Peter, a fisherman who lacked education, was impetuous and little changed by his years with Jesus, suddenly was a new creature and began seeing miracles occur around him that included healing the infirm, giving sight to the blind, casting out demons and even raising the dead to new life. Even after Peter did the unbelievable—denying any connection to Jesus, still the Spirit was willing to use this frail servant to do mighty works in the name of the Lord. Two months after his denial of Jesus, Peter spoke before the masses with such fervor that 3,000 people accepted faith in Jesus Christ on a single day. I have always been proud of the fact that among the mentioned 3,000 new believers that day there were Arabs.

So we Christian Arabs in the Middle East trace our lineage in the Church back to the time of Christ. Ever since those days Arab-Christians have lived in the Middle East. When Islamic rule came many centuries later, Christians became a minority in the region and lived under the *dimma* system that defined the rights of minorities of the monotheistic religions (Christians and also the Jews). The lives of

Christians were sometimes comfortable and sometimes hard to bear depending on the attitude of the current ruling caliph.

Despite the oppressions they had to face over the ages, many Arab Christians held fast to the faith of their ancestors, though there were others who couldn't bear the pressure and chose the easy way of converting to Islam. Today Christians remain a minority in the Middle East, with some fifteen million Christians in the region with the majority of twelve million of them living in Egypt, while the rest are scattered throughout Iraq, Syria, Jordan, Lebanon, Israel and Palestine.

It behooves us as Arab Evangelicals not to distance ourselves from the Arab-Christian community or ignore the history of Arab Christians who have maintained a presence here for 2,000 years. We need to build the community as a whole and the Evangelical community in particular.

Evangelicals have a tendency to Americanize or Westernize the Arab-Christian church. A balance should be made between being an integral part of the Arab church in the Middle East and developing relationships (and influences that come as a result of that) from the church in the West.

The Middle East in general and the historical land of Israel/Palestine in particular are special in that they are the birthplace of the monotheistic religions. The land of Israel (Jerusalem, Jericho, Hebron, Shiloh) are considered the birthplace of Judaism. That small and narrow strip of land is also considered the birthplace of Christianity (Jerusalem, Bethlehem, Tiberias, Nazareth), while the Arab Peninsula is the birthplace of Islam.

A witness for this amazing history can be found in archeological excavations around the country. These stones remind the world of the divine revelation in this part of the world. Every Christian visitor to our small country sees for themselves the locale where Jesus was born, lived, acted, taught, was put on the cross and killed, rose from death and ascended to heaven. All around the country, archeological excavations constantly expose stones that affirm and document the divine presence in this locale for thousands of years. These dusty stones tell the stories that millions of believers worldwide have been affected by. Hundreds of thousands of Christian pilgrims come each year to the Holy Land and spend days visiting religious and archeological sites in order to relive the stories of the Bible and actually walk on the stones where Jesus walked. Yet local Christians often complain that these pilgrims do little to visit or build relationships with the "living stones" whose homeland is in Israel.

The New Testament depicts the Church with various images—like the body of the Messiah, with Jesus being the head and the believers being his body. Other metaphors include the building of God, a herd of sheep whose Shepherd is Jesus, the shield of God, the bride of the Messiah and others.

In the illustration of the church or the congregation as a building of God, the stones are those of living stones (the believers). An important part of building is its foundation, being strongly rooted so that its stones stick to each other with special glue. Thus it is natural to see the believers in church as siblings, bound to one another through the blood shed on the cross—therefore the bond is very strong.

The fact that Christian believers—pilgrims—are not interested in any connection to local believers causes disappointment. The presence of such connections hold special significance to Arab Christians because of their situation as a minority and because of their difficulties in living in a land filled with hostilities. Also, there is the fact that many Christian pilgrims sympathize and admire (and often support) Israel and Jews, wherever they are.

Many local Christian clergy remind their Western Christian audiences of the "living stones" and urge Western churches to maintain close relationships with the "living stones" in the Holy Land. Since I am involved in a church and Christian school in Nazareth, I have the opportunity to develop relationships with Western Christians. When these relationships are based on mutual coöperation according to need and not on unilateral relationships that have the Western side giving and the locals just receiving, then these relationships can develop in an amazing way for shared enrichment.

The Christian minority in the Holy land expect the Christians of the world to be aware of their existence as a minority presence in the land. Several times I have met Christians around the world who had no clue about our very existence in the land. A pastor of a church with 7,000 believers in the U.S. explained to me that we were "under the radar of the American public." We don't expect political or economic patronizing but we do expect support so we can continue to live in the land where our Lord chose to be born, live, die and rise again from the dead.

Actually through the years, Western churches have established schools, hospitals, colleges and old people's homes here. Such relationships tend to foster dependency or even a patronizing gap in expectations, since the universal principle applies that the one with the money can also dictate. At times there have been Christian workers who have raised funds abroad based on misinformation or pandering to Western audiences. This brings either a lack of control or an improper use of donated funds.

Fortunately there have been many positive and productive relationships and partnerships between Christians here and around the world. I have been connected to Christians from abroad who have lived and worked in Nazareth, leaving behind a comfortable life in the West to do everything possible to serve the Lord here in the Holy Land. Among these is the late Swiss doctor Hans Bernath who spent more than 40 years with his family, serving the people of Nazareth in the Scottish hospital. His gentleness, humility and personal sacrifices for others will long be remembered. Dr. Bernath, a short man with tough features and dark skin, first came to this country during World War II with the Red Cross. Afterwards he returned and served faithfully until his retirement. He was known far and wide for his work as a surgeon and director of a central hospital built with some of the carpentry in various hospital departments done with his own hands.

Understanding that we are all living stones is a vital concept. First, we must be worthy to be called that. Being a nominal or a cultural Christian is not enough. As living stones we are members of the body of the Lord in his own hometown and thus should have the characteristics that honor that role. This includes developing a purpose-driven life, coöperation, love for the community and a servant heart.

7

Biblical Metaphors for Our Ministry

Belonging to the tiny Arab Christian Evangelical community in Israel is a peculiar situation. It means living as an Evangelical minority among Christians, a Christian minority among Muslim Arabs, and as an Arab minority among the Jewish Israelis in Israel. To add to the complication, I am an Israeli citizen but also a Palestinian and my country of residence is in a bitter struggle with my people. With all these complicated conflicting sub identities and affiliations, it is no wonder that we are unable to categorize our entity in a simple manner.

The Bible provides several metaphors for the ministry of the Disciples of Christ. One is being **salt** (Mt 5:13). A small amount of salt gives taste to food as well as preserves it. Another is **light** (Mt 5:14, a metaphor that Jesus used for himself too) casting away the darkness of the world. Disciples are asked to be **ambassadors** (2 Co 5:20), representing and bringing forth the message of their sender. In the great commandment the disciples are also required to be **witnesses** (Ac 1:8). As those that have witnessed the grace of God they will tell by their deeds, words or even presence and perseverance about that grace.

We can also take inspiration from the builders in Nehemiah's days. Our ministry requires **building** on the one hand and **fighting** on the other. So we are like the builders who joined Nehemiah in rebuilding Jerusalem after they returned to the ruined city—they reconstructed the walls with one hand, holding a sword for protection in the other (Neh 4:17).

I believe our ministry in this setting can be reflected in such a metaphor. Sometimes our ministry is proactive—including rebuking the darkness and taking a prophetic position and thus resembling the light, while in other cases we are "merely" witnesses. As a tiny minority in a land filled with conflicts and contradictions we largely serve as witnesses. We have seen the truth and we tell about it when we can, but we have to express restraint and keep silent when our being a minority causes us to be attacked—and even our silence is a witness.

The next chapters will describe the layers of this peculiarity of our presence and the role we take in it. I could be wearing the hat of the Arab treated badly in the Jewish country, trying to sort out the correct reaction as a disciple of Christ. Or I might be wearing the hat of a Christian Arab being forced to leave the Holy Land and how we deal with this threat in a way that honors God too.

In some cases we act as builders, in others as salt and sometimes as witnesses.

8

Building What?

One of the metaphors of our ministry is that of builders, as in the time of the prophet Nehemiah. As followers of Christ in this land filled with holy sites and the stones where Jesus walked, we are called to be builders. However we are builders of living stones.

Today we are involved in building protective walls around the Evangelical community. Our role in the rebuilding process seems to involve encouraging the faithful, urging them to persevere in a purpose-driven life. To do this we endeavor to build up the community in their faith, helping them to listen to God's call in the midst of hostile surroundings by establishing support systems and organizations that can build the community and also by establishing relationships with the Evangelical church worldwide.

Not only do these protective walls need to be high and strong, but bridges of understanding and reconciliation are needed. The sword in the one hand is not one that kills, but is only brandished in an effort to protect against enemy-led schemes and actions, guarding the community from prejudice in this setting overflowing with domestic violence, marginalization and stereotypes.

Building the walls means simply building the church. We hold tight to the truth that "Except the Lord builds the house, they labor in vain that build it: except the Lord keep the city, the watchman waketh but in vain"(Ps 127:1). God is the true builder but we are privileged to work with the Lord. "For we are laborers together with God: ye are

God's husbandry, ye are God's building (1 Co 3:9).

Building the church together with the Lord involves building up individuals in the church. This includes not only discipleship and teaching in the narrow perspective, but also comprehensively dealing with all aspects of life: spiritual, psychological and physical. It includes education, reconciliation, legal aid and health care. Thus I feel privileged to be involved in the ministry of building up the Arab-Palestinian-Israeli-Christian-Evangelical community in Nazareth, Israel, where clashing identities and pressures in our community demand that we work on reconciliation between Arabs and Jews.

One way the underprivileged Arab community, of which I am part, can close the gap is through education. Thus our small Evangelical community is concentrating on forming institutions and structures of accountability that requires expertise, discernment and knowledge.

The years 1995 and 1996 were years of beginnings. It was during these two years that I joined a team of local and Western Christian believers in establishing the "Nazareth Village" and at the same time became involved with others in establishing the local Baptist church in Nazareth. Like many other churches, this church came about as a result of a split. Yet at the time it created in us such enthusiasm to build up this great place of worship with lovely people, that the Lord has used and we hope the Lord will continue to use it in a mighty way for the Lord's glory in the coming years here in Nazareth.

Most Evangelical churches in the country were planted by missionaries from abroad (generally America), but by now the majority of these American missionaries have left Israel, leaving these churches in the hands of indigenous leaders. Of course, these American missionaries left their mark and influence on these churches. The farther removed these churches are from the foreign missionary generation, the more local customs influence these church communities. Therefore, today we find an interesting process of crystallizing the local identity, whether this be Jordanian, Egyptian, West Bank Arab Evangelical churches or the Messianic congregations in Israel with which the Arab-Christian communities enjoy a good relationship.

Beyond this, there is the impact on the local churches by what is happening in the broader Christian churches from other denominations, including a new involvement in community matters, which traditionally the Evangelical churches refrained from getting involved, feeling their energies should be focused solely on spiritual matters. This led, in 2005, to an initiative to form an Evangelical convention that would serve as an umbrella organization for Evangelical churches and para-churches in Israel.

This initiative centered on creating a balanced system that would take all "church families," as they were called, into consideration so that Evangelicals from different denominations could come together under the banner of Christ. Evangelicals from the West find it odd that Christian Brethren and Assemblies of God, for example, here in Israel work together in joint ministry. We explain to them that with the challenges and small numbers we have, no one can afford to remain isolated within their strict denominational boundaries.

Building was done not only in church life but also in education.

It was natural that churches in Europe and America would want to be active in the Holy Land—the birthplace of our Savior. This led to a plethora of church-related projects, like hospitals, schools, covenants, orphanages and churches from every area of Christendom.

These institutions brought health and education to the local people along with their Western influence. Most of the students who studied in their schools in the beginning were Christians and they received a remarkable education so today they enjoy a high percentage of academic positions throughout the whole country.

Traditionally Muslims in the Middle East have called Christians and Jews the "people of the Book" because of their deep respect for their Scriptures—the Old and New Testaments. The educational achievements of the Christian community have also given them stature throughout the Middle East where they are seen as generally academic high achievers.

Christian schools in Israel continue to maintain this heritage and reputation so schools like St. Joseph (Al Motran), the Nazareth Baptist School and the Orthodox school in Haifa are renowned throughout the country. This has led to a healthy competition which keeps everyone on their toes. Our school, for example, has been doing remarkably well with notable achievements in an old campus on less than an acre of land with 800 students and with another 200 students in an even older rented facility nearby. My big challenge will be to move our school to the next level with a new campus.

High achieving parents want their children to study at these schools and do everything possible to help their offspring succeed in their studies. As the general director of a prestigious school I daily field phone calls from people who try to convince me to accept their child in our school—a task that is becoming burdensome to me.

The Catholic schools like the Salvatory Sisters school, St. Joseph nuns' school, Don Bosco and the Franciscan school in Nazareth or the Carmelite school and St. John's in Haifa and Mar Elias in Ibbilin also compete to be regarded as the best schools in the land.

In light of the success of the Christians schools in Israel and the failures of the whole Israeli educational system in the last few years, it would seem useful should the leaders of the educational system conduct studies into the phenomenal success of Christian schools instead of reaching out to distant places to learn from their experience—but this would require some humility on the part of the Israeli authorities, a trait for which they are not noted. It goes against their grain that as an, albeit clandestine, nuclear power and the "only democracy in the Middle East," with a lot of high tech industry, to want to learn from Arabs, especially Christian Arabs.

We Christians have much for which to be grateful for. This foreign intervention on our behalf has proven to be a long-term blessing that has given a better quality of life to all the residents of this nation. To counter this boon, this highly educated Christian populace in Israel and the occupied territories has produced a low birth rate, plus a facility for emigration out of this hostile climate, which has reduced the Christian presence in this country drastically. Still, education remains an important tool for the Christian community.

In my own nuclear family, composed of two siblings, we and our spouses all have master's degrees or are currently pursuing one. In my extended family, two aunts and a cousin have earned PhDs. When I graduated from high school 27 years ago our school had an exceptionally high number of graduates admitted to university.

Now, with the recognition that higher education is absolutely vital for success in our economic situation, as general director of this school, I have to demand even more from our students if we are to remain competitive with other schools in the country. Thus we constantly add new programs and encourage our students to participate in academic contests such as national competitions in mathematics, physics, astronomy, building robots and developing economic models managed by the students. This, in addition to courses in building internet networks for computer companies, musical bands, English competitions, student exchanges with schools abroad, ballet dancing, competitive sports—the list goes on. These programs turn our school into a veritable ant house with students scurrying around completing different activities in order to enrich their chances at success in a situation that puts high demands on young Arabs living in most troubled times.

As Arab Christian believers we must do all we can to facilitate the education and nurture of our Christian youth and I certainly put my energies into keeping Nazareth Baptist School standards high in order to provide an excellent educational experience for our community—Christian and Muslim. We are gratified that many of our alumni are now stationed in key positions in our society, contributing to its general welfare— which is all due to the sacrificial giving of Western Christian churches that began these schools here, many over a century ago. The fruit of this planting goes on being harvested today by the Arab-Christian community which enjoys the highest ratio of an educated populace in the whole of Israeli society.

A good education provides students with tools to make a positive contribution to society. Christian ministries have done the best to make that happen in the Middle East—as they have done around the world. As salt and light we are asked to be positive factors in Arab society. But I have repeatedly tried to impress on our staff that a superb academic education must be accompanied with teaching values and being living examples for our students if we are not going to fill their brains with formulas and information but leave their hearts empty of compassion and love for their neighbor.

Christian Evangelicals in Israel only number some 5,000 people, but they are an active and renewed body of believers as was recently illustrated when a few years ago an official decided to organize a program to teach Christian education in Arab schools in Israel for Christians. A committee was formed to put together such a program with the chair being a Greek-Catholic priest. He chose several priests and pastors to develop the curriculum—without any input from the Evangelical community of believers.

Two Evangelical Biblical scholars reviewed the proposed curriculum and felt it wasn't a suitable expression of our faith since it excluded our point of view. To counter this "claimed" monopoly on the Christian faith, we formed a committee of Evangelicals to try to deal with the issue. However no solution was found. We have used different channels in order to open a dialogue with other churches, in vain. We contemplated appealing to the Supreme Court on this issue of discrimination, but then felt it would be a bad testimony to the cause of Christ should Christian denominations face each other in the Israeli court system. We then decided to appeal to the Supreme Court against the ministry of education—an issue that is still pending.

Nazareth is a wonderful place to pursue a good education, for after all it was here that our Savior grew in wisdom, grace and stature before God and the community. It is also a privilege to be part of a group of Christian believers (Catholic, Baptist, Orthodox, Mennonite, Anglican and Brethren) from Nazareth and around the world who felt called to create a replica of the first century village of Nazareth

The dream originated with Dr. Nakhle Bishara, a Greek Orthodox eighth generation Nazarene who had watched pilgrims stream through Nazareth to absorb the air of the town where Christ grew up. He realized many were disappointed to find few vestiges of anything that resembled the town where Jesus lived, for today Nazareth is a hilly, dusty town with crowded streets and heavy traffic.

In 1995 Dr. Nakhle shared this dream with Mike Hostetler, an American Mennonite film producer who visited Nazareth to make a film about the town. Mike was captivated by this dream and asked permission to take it further. Dr. Nakhle was then the medical director of Nazareth Hospital that had been established by the Edinburgh Medical Mission society. The society had owned some eight acres of land near the hospital for over a century which they had planned to use for various projects— either expanding the hospital or perhaps building a hotel for pilgrims. But none of these plans had materialized and it appeared that God had saved this plot for a new project.

In the end it seemed a natural fit to choose that specific land for a museum/village. Located a few hundred yards from the Annunciation Church built on the site where the house of Mary and Joseph is said to have existed, it was also the only land preserved all those years with nothing on it. In fact, it was the only plot of vacant land available inside the city limits.

Mike went to meet the Scotch directors of the society who immediately agreed to the project and even contributed funds to get it started. At this stage I joined the steering committee formed of local residents and internationals. We conducted a serious feasibility study that showed that the idea to be viable and then went on planning and praying.

One day and while we were in those beginning stages, an archeologist was wandering on the land with Mike when he suddenly came across a curved stone jutting out of the mountainside. Bending to pick it up, he was dumbfounded to realize he had stumbled on a first century wine press. We were all excited to see Mark 12:1 come true before our own eyes. On this piece of land in Nazareth where Jesus probably played as a young boy we could envision a vineyard, a wall, a pit, a wine press and a watch tower. They were all there. We saw this as a divine sign of the hand of God to go forward.

A team was formed to research the land, clear it of debris that had accumulated over the centuries, and raise the necessary support with the help of various religious and community leaders. There was much to be done: an organizational structure needed to be established, procedures agreed to, building permission plus fund-raising. For three years we planned and waited on the Lord for guidance, meeting every Tuesday evening to encourage each other, oversee the process and progress, pray and discuss and wait for the Lord to provide the means for starting such an ambitious project. We had a strong sense of mission and a zeal to glorify Jesus in his own hometown.

Amazingly enough, the piece of land where Nazareth Village was established used to be the place I spent hours playing soccer as a child. I even recall sitting on what turned out to be the ancient winepress to rest during our pickup games in that vacant plot. It was scary, but at times we found drug needles near there because the nocturnal activity was obviously taken over by addicts and others who used the area for their own nefarious purposes, which obviously wasn't pleasing to the Lord. It now feels as though the Lord has redeemed this land where the Nazareth Village was created for purposes that glorify God's name.

Today the Nazareth Village tells Jesus' story to thousands of visitors from all backgrounds and countries. It is a living museum with displays which illustrate how life was lived in Christ's day. Through the agricultural displays, the winepress, the synagogue, the reconstructed houses and olive press it shows the environment from which Jesus created his parables.

Nazareth Village has become a wonderful resource and tool for the Christian community creating a place for connecting the worldwide church to local believers in Nazareth. Where better place in the world to visit should one want to know more about Jesus than Nazareth? It has been a privilege for me to have the opportunity to be part of the team that built such a lovely place that could be an answer to truth seekers.

Being involved in these building ventures in Nazareth and Galilee has given us a sweet taste of achievement in the midst of the winds of hatred, bigotry and racism that infect this troubled land.

9

Surviving Anti-Arab Sentiment

These are difficult days to be an Arab—with people like Osama bin Laden, Muammar Qaddafi, Hosni Mubarak and others making Arabs look bad in the eyes of the world—and not doing much for our own self-esteem either. Unfortunately, Arabs around the world are also spearheading anti-American sentiment. So this means Arabs are constantly faced with having to overcome stereotypes and negative thinking about them. This anti-Arab sentiment has different levels that we have no choice but to tackle.

One is the **general anti-Arab** sentiment we face because of the bad reputation Arab people have among the nations. Another has an additional despised component: Palestinian. It is the **anti-Palestinian Arab** prejudice (mainly against those living in the West Bank and Gaza that were occupied in 1967). Being Arab is difficult, but being a Palestinian Arab compounds this in light of the Israeli-Palestinian conflict. The third anti-Arab sentiment relates to us as **Arab Palestinians who live in Israel** and enjoy Israel's citizenship.

We are not stigmatized with the general Arab label nor with the "Palestinian" addition only, but with another component. As Israeli citizens we are expected to be "loyal" to Israel and abide by its policies. However, as Palestinians we have sympathy for our neighbors in the West Bank and Gaza as well as those Palestinian refugees around the world and we pray and hope for a just solution to their situation. This makes it inevitable that we vocally oppose discriminatory policies of the Israeli government concerning the

Palestinians that foments and strengthens anti-Arab sentiment.

How do you reflect Christ and honor him in such situations? Sometimes it requires opposition to these stereotypes or anti-Arab sentiments or acts of prejudice by pointing to the oppressor and demanding that justice be done. Sometimes it requires taking a passive and peaceful attitude. Sometimes you are "just" a witness while at other times light exposing the hatred and bigotry.

I have been involved in such *general* anti-Arab sentiments. When the Twin Towers was attacked in New York I was attending a conference on freedom of religion for Christian lawyers from all over Europe being held in Sesembra on the shores of the Atlantic Ocean in south Portugal. The conference organizers and many of the attendees had known me personally for years and some had visited and stayed at my home in Nazareth. They tried to assuage my guilt at being part of a world that had brought about this senseless attack; nevertheless I felt obligated to apologize on the behalf of those of my "tribe" who had done such an unjustifiable act.

My American friends at the conference gave me authentic support and tried to encourage me knowing my life would henceforth be complicated with "special" tight scrutiny any time I traveled by air. In fact, returning from this conference, like for many around the world, including my sister who happened to be taking a course just then in Baltimore, getting back home proved to be a trial by fire.

I did not need to wait long to realize that an Arab as such was becoming a threatening word in the West. Two days later, after the conference ended, I was subjected to "special" tight scrutiny at Lisbon airport. Such treatment has subsequently repeated itself in different airports over and over again. Arriving in Zurich from Lisbon on the night of September 13th, I learned the Israeli security had canceled the Swiss Air flight to Israel. The next flight to Tel Aviv would not leave until the next morning—and the ticketing clerk announced sweetly that Swiss Air was not obliged to provide lodging for me since the flight was canceled by the Israeli security. I would have to make my own arrangements for lodging that night.

By then it was ten o'clock at night and I preferred to feel victimized and indulge in self pity by sleeping on one of the wooden benches in the airport—which felt like a better option than carrying my heavy luggage out of the airport to the city and waste a good number of Swiss francs on a couple of hours sleep in a hotel. I related to the homeless that night in Zurich airport and it wasn't too uncomfortable until the cleaning lady decided she needed to sweep precisely under the bench I was using at 4:30 that morning. My family was relieved when I arrived home, especially since my sister got stuck in Baltimore until the air restrictions were removed ten days later.

Since then I have experienced rejection and suspicion towards me as an Arab, but I discovered that one can overcome preconceived ideas by developing open and good relationships with folk from all over the world. It remains a challenge to show everyone respect and equality, even when there are deep wounds to overcome, but as Christians we are to show Christ's love to all those around us—enemies and friends. Stooping to labeling and exclusivism does not reflect the mind of Christ.

Over the years we have entertained those from abroad who with tears have admitted preconceived prejudices they've discovered were based on misinformation. Spending time with Arab-Christians is an important element is reversing these wrongful feelings which behooves us as Arab-Christians in Nazareth to be ever kind, open and loving to all who come to visit us in the Holy Land.

Groups of Western students who arrive for exchange programs with students of their age in Nazareth have often expressed similar feelings. As Christians who follow the Bible we are asked to be open to the creation of God. If Christians were to cling to stereotypes and false perceptions, then the nations of the world would not have been reached by the Gospel brought to them by those who crossed cultural barriers. Godly and courageous people have sacrificed their comfort and their lives to reach out with the Good News to cannibals and iso-lated violent tribes.

We sometimes close ourselves in a ghetto-like society of Christian believers of our own type instead of going out and meeting others from different backgrounds and checking where such stereotypes come from. We are always enriched by such encounters.

It seems apparent that the general mindset towards the Arab image in the world will not change in the near future, but we as Christians can work along the margins with individuals to improve this attitude. I am convinced the change in perceptions will occur as the actions of Arabs change and they begin to contribute positively to the world civilization.

As Christian believers we are required to look at our neighbors around the world through Christ's point of view—without prejudice or stereotypes. He accepted everyone as God's creations and sinners needing God's salvation. Jesus treated everyone from different backgrounds with the same love and forgiveness. He cared about Jews, Samaritans, lepers, religious people and despised tax collectors with the same compassion. So today Christ would surely care about Arabs and make them feel accepted. As Christians we can do nothing less

My constituency is that of the Arab people and besides being respectful to the symbols of the others I think it is important to express our views in a proper and loving manner. A few years ago I participated in an international conference where the internationals were asked to hold the flags of their countries during a fund-raising photo op. I was given the Israeli flag in the parade.

For me it was a dilemma. My people were fighting my country. Their symbols do not represent me. I knew that if a photo of me holding the flag was published, it would hurt people from my community, especially those who had suffered greatly as a result of the establishment of Israel. It would also cause me to lose my credibility. I declined and another arrangement was made.

The general anti-Arab sentiment can't be disconnected from anti-Islamic feelings around the world. Ironically these anti-Islamic sentiments contribute to what I suffer as an Arab Christian. As a Christian community, we have lived among Muslims all our lives. I lived with Muslims in the dorms at the university and count several

Muslims among my circle of friends. As a child I had Muslims in my circle of playmates for we have always had Muslim neighbors.

My mother tells me that when I was young I would come home and swear (give oath) on the "Mus-haf" (the Koran). This was the level of engagement we as Christians had and still have with our Muslims neighbors. As a minority among them, we had the privilege of learning about their religion and their religious practices. Almost all Arab Christians I know are experts on Muslims—just because we grew up with them.

Unlike life in the West where a person can be secular and where people live individualistically, in the Middle East everybody belongs to a faith group and people lead their lives in a community and share their lives with the others in their communities. In light of this, Islam and its practices and how Muslims (in Israel at least) perceive it and practice their faith is something we grow up with. Islam is thus closely related to our Arab identity, even for Christians like me for it is a central part of our culture.

Islam was mostly an unknown in the West until the attack on the Twin Towers. The fanatic lunatic Muslim leader Osama bin Laden was little regarded among people around the world until then—even though he was on the Most Wanted list for years.

Westerners sometimes find it strange to realize that in calling a person to a new life in Christ in our Arab milieu, it is necessary to address the influence of Islam on our culture. Some might reject this out of hand and see it as blasphemy because many in the West regard Islam as a man-made religion not derived from the true God. But regardless of one's perspective on Islam, it is vital to address it as a rising and dominant part of the culture I live in.

I was, of course, raised as a Christian believer and firmly believe in the Christian doctrines which I will not compromise just to please the Muslim majority. Yet I believe we should respect the Muslim faith and practices, just as we ask Muslims to respect our faith, not only in the West where they are a minority but in the East, too. Mutuality should be firmly demanded from Muslims as a basis to any dialogue. If Muslims are given the right to build mosques in Los Angeles,

Rome, Copenhagen and Nazareth then Christians should be given permission to build churches in Mecca, Kabul, Dubai and Kuala Lumpur. Furthermore, as Muslims are given the right to win converts for Islam in the West in the name of the freedom of religion, then this right should be extended to Christians in Muslim countries.

It is my conviction that Christian Arabs can be a bridge to the Muslim world. Our familiarity with the Islamic culture is added to our mastery of the Arabic language—fundamental in Islam—which is our own language, too. We know the mentality, customs, culture and fundamentals of their faith and can be a resource for dialogue between religions. We are also in a position to reach out to them in the love of Christ

The message of Christ's love that the Holy Spirit took to the nations in the first century delivered by a bunch of simple fishermen changed the whole known world at that time. It has the same power today—but stumbling blocks do spring up. Some Muslims think an offensive cartoon published a few years ago in Denmark was drawn by Christians, therefore these Muslims are not open to hear any message (Gospel message or other) coming from the West.

They also tend to identify ex-President George Bush and his policies around the world with Christianity—which makes them anti-Christian because of their disapproval of his choices. Too, the continued support the West gives to Israel is seen as an act against Arabs and Islam since it created the Palestinian problem. Muslims look negatively on Christianity as they identify policies of Western governments as well as positions of religious figures (including the American Evangelical right-wing and pro-Israeli leaders) as identical with what Christianity has to offer.

It is important to respect the Muslims' faith and come to agreement with the moderates among them, giving them a reason to seek peace and abide in it through suppression of the forces that are trying to disturb the world balance. This attitude works in Turkey which is enjoying fruitful relations with the West and is even looking to join the European Union.

Another way to undermine fanatic Islamicism is by seeking a true and functional solution to the core conflict of the East-West: the Palestinian issue. A just solution for the Palestinians will bring a change to the cloudy atmosphere in the region by bringing a refreshing wind. Through that, it will be possible to strengthen the moderate line among the Muslims, but it is important to act fast before it is too late.

The language component of my Arab identity is an important one for it allows an Arab-Christian voice be heard in Arabic in the Middle East. When the Islam voice is so prominent and loud in the Middle East, it is vital to balance this with a genuine Arab-Christian voice informed by the Bible and the common Christian heritage of the Arabs. Arab Christians have contributed to the literature, philosophy and arts in Arabic in the past and it is important that this Christian voice continue to be heard in the language of the Koran.

My own efforts have included contributing articles in Arabic to the general press and various websites as well as Evangelical organs where I've commented on society and church issues. I have also written a booklet called "Who are the Arab Evangelicals in Israel?" and feel privileged to answer this calling to contribute to the building of the Evangelical community in our country through educating by writing in the language of the region—Arabic.

10

Anti-Palestinian Arab Sentiments

Another layer of anti-Arab sentiments that we have to deal with is prejudice specifically against Arab Palestinians outside Israel (as the Palestinian Arabs like myself are a special category to be addressed in the next chapter).

It is interesting to note that dates of birth here have meanings. One of my friends in Nazareth was born in Jerusalem on the actual date of the occupation in 1967—one of the darkest days in the history of the Palestinians. On the other hand, my brother was born on the 27th of December. We met to celebrate his 40th birthday on the day Israel started the war in Gaza in 2007. My birthday falls on the day of the 1973 war, although I was born exactly eight years before it. My cousin who passed away on the first day of 2010, aged 48, was an Arab nationalist and active politically. Ironically, he was born on the day of the Israeli independence.

One can't talk about the Palestinian issue without mentioning the suffering Palestinians have faced since hundreds of thousands became refugees in 1948, losing their homes and homeland. Others lost their land and freedom and have lived under occupation for years. This anguish has generated much sympathy for the Palestinian cause around the world. Our current problems began over a century ago and have wrought much distress for both the Israelis and the Palestinians.

Jesus preached a message of transformation that would one day produce peace, security and development. Many Palestinian Christians feel they are excluded from this design for humanity. I am confident the Lord had a plan for me that included being raised here in Palestine, yet seeing the difficulties my people have suffered over the years, I long for the day when peace and prosperity are part of God's plan for Palestinians as well.

Some Christian believers see nations through the lens of eternal salvation for individuals only. I believe the Lord's will is broader and includes establishing the kingdom of God on earth, as well. God wishes all to live according to God's values, so they will lead godly lives knowing Christ as Lord and Savior. God wants us to live in social justice, reconciliation and also prosperity. I believe firmly that God wants all peoples to enjoy fine arts, music and sports. After all, aren't we all God's creation, created in God's image?

Some wonder how I can be both an Evangelical and a Palestinian who loves my people. The difficulty comes from a common view among many Evangelicals that claims the current state of Israel is a fulfillment of prophecy foreshadowing the Second Coming of Christ. Which brings us to the question: What about the Palestinians, the natives? Are they just an obstacle to God's plans?

Nobody (including Israel) has the right to act in contradiction to the Biblical principles of compassion, mercy, justice and equality. The bitter conflict between the Israelis and the Palestinians has put both peoples in difficult situations. At different stages, both groups were forced to act in a brutal way—and both have dehumanized each other.

God created us in order that we might glorify God. Both Israelis and Palestinians have failed to do that. I can only cry for the Palestinians and pray their agony will soon end. I cannot accept those who only talk about the so-called cruelty, brutality and violence of the Palestinians without ascribing the same behavior to the Israelis. I do pray for a change in the course of history so both sides might have the opportunity to live peacefully with one another.

Both sides have made bitter mistakes and have been brutal towards the other. Reconciliation is required for both. Justice is needed for both. As Christians we must take a prophetic stance condemning sinful behavior and not hide behind eschatological schemes.

Living in Jerusalem I witnessed this suffering while working as an Arab-Palestinian lawyer there. I have also been to the military court in the West Bank where I saw the cruel way in which Palestinians are treated there. Military rules have been imposed on them so that disclosures, curfews, sieges and such behavior restrict and limit the rights of the occupied.

There are 1.4 million Muslim Palestinians living in difficult circumstances in Gaza—plus a small community of a few thousand Christians as well, including less than a hundred Evangelicals. The pastor of the only Evangelical church in Gaza is a Fuller Seminary graduate with an American green card who chose to return to Gaza to serve the local Evangelical church there—one of the few lighthouses in the dark, miserable life in Gaza. In the midst of hatred he reflects the love of Christ to those around him. A while back the pastor's wife, a Jordanian, went to visit her parents in Jordan with her newborn baby. The Israelis refused to let her return home.

At that point we launched a campaign on a small website we run in English asking our readers to send letters of protest to Israeli embassies around the world. The Israelis were unmoved and refused to grant her permission to return to her husband in Gaza. What basic logic prevailed on them to prohibit a young, defenseless mother and wife of this Evangelical pastor to return to one of the more miserable places on earth? Only when she appealed to the Supreme Court in Israel did the authorities agree to allow her to come back.

As a lawyer I have represented many Gaza residents in cases against their employees in Israel for industrial accidents that happened to them while working there. Basic workers' compensation was denied them until expensive legal pressure was brought to bear to give them the rights they deserved for their work-related injuries. There were various loopholes the employers employed, but mainly it was due to the fact that they knew those living in Gaza had little recourse to the Israeli courts and so denied them their lawful rights as long as they could get away with this type of behavior.

Workers living in Gaza now need a special permit to enter Israel in order to get to court or for a medical examination. In addition, filing complaints and claims requires substantial upfront money for court fees and financial guarantees plus expert medical witnesses—all that at a time when the situation in Gaza is economically perilous, so such sums of money aren't available. Even when they overcome such obstacles and succeed in court, still collecting judgments is very difficult.

The life of those in Gaza is barely bearable. Everyone there has a life tinged with personal tragedy. Occupation can never be enlightened and I have witnessed physical torture in addition to the daily difficulties of surviving there. At the end of my study in Jerusalem, I accompanied an American friend serving with the Baptist mission to the police station in Jerusalem so he could file a complaint about the theft of his car. While I waited outside when he was filling out the necessary papers, I saw the Israeli police haul a young Palestinian man into the station for questioning. Some 15 minutes later he was dragged out of the room, blood covering his face. The policemen didn't notice me there and I later sent a letter reporting the incident to a local Hebrew newspaper where it was published. No one ever followed up nor appeared to inquire about this further—just another normal police day.

I would have expected this anti-Arab Palestinian sentiment be opposed by Christians everywhere; however, this is not the case. The relationship of American Evangelicals to the Palestinian Evangelicals borders on bizarre. The difficulties seem to have evolved out of doctrines that imply God needs our help to bring on the Second Coming of Christ and establish the millennium of peace. Unfortunately these views are based not on facts and good biblical scholarship, but on rantings and ravings of some who feel it is necessary to love and support Jews in general and Messianic Jews in particular. Arab-Christians in Israel are apparently dispensable items.

When both sides get to know each other and a relationship develops built upon partnership, there is a good chance for ministry in the service of the Lord. But too often we have encountered an almost patronizing attitude from Americans who seem uninterested in knowing anything about us, our history in the Holy Land or our efforts to serve the Christian community in Israel.

Many Evangelical leaders we have met even seem to resent our presence in the Holy Land, because it doesn't mesh with their ideas of what should be. Some come up with a simplistic analysis of what is happening there and don't want to be disturbed with the true facts of the matter, so our presence becomes an embarrassment.

Most Evangelicals we encounter can't fit Palestinian Christians or Evangelical Palestinians into their equation, so our existence seems to be a stumbling block to them. I have met some who are dumbfounded and in tears when they learn there is an Evangelical Christian church in Palestine that has been serving the Lord faithfully in difficult situations down through the centuries.

The Bible is full of verses that point to the need of compassion, mercy and justice. Even the strongest supporters of Israel have to confess that injustice was done to the Palestinians by Israel in the long years of the occupation. The Palestinians were not passive during those years and they were and still are trying to get revenge on the Israelis for this mistreatment. However this does not exempt the Israelis with their power base from doing the right thing towards their neighbors.

Many Evangelicals concentrate on the vision of the "dry bones" in Ezekiel in order to base their argument about the return of the Jewish people to their own country; however there are commands throughout the Old Testament that call for them to share the land with those who are living among them.

Abraham, the patriarch, was given a divine promise concerning the land, yet he insisted on paying for the land he wanted allocated for Sarah's tomb in the Cave of Machpela in Hebron—despite the generosity of the local people who wanted to give it to them freely. Maybe he was hinting to the new generations that they should be gracious themselves with the natives of the place too?

11

Prejudice Against Palestinian Israelis

The third layer of anti-Arab sentiments that we deal with relates to my specific situation as an Arab-Palestinian minority in Israel. Roughly speaking there are three groups of Palestinians. Those in the lands occupied in 1967 by Israel (the West Bank and Gaza). These are demanding the end of occupation and establishment of a Palestinian state. The second are Palestinian refugees (or descendants of such refugees) scattered in neighboring Arab countries (like Lebanon, Syria and Jordan) and in the West. The main thrust of this group is the right to return to the places they were displaced from or at least the right to receive reasonable compensation for their lost property. The third is that of Arab Palestinians who did not become refugees but stayed in their homes in 1948, found themselves in the state of Israel and were granted Israeli citizenship. This is the group I am part of.

Our group is in a sensitive and interesting situation. We are Israeli citizens but are Arabs in a Jewish country where our people are in conflict with our country. Israel's dealings with the Arab countries and with the Palestinian people directly impact their dealings with us. We are expected to give total loyalty, but our hearts are divided as we sympathize with our people. We are not equal citizens and naturally we feel aliens in our own land because of Israel's Jewish nature.

What is the appropriate Christian response to these sentiments and complications?

This difficulty starts from the core of the Jewish state, Israel: the Law of Return gives every Jew worldwide the right to make *aliya* and arrive in Israel as a newcomer and obtain all the rights reserved for citizens. On the other hand the indigenous people who have lived in Israel/Palestine for centuries are second-class citizens and others are deprived of their homeland.

This was illustrated recently in an amusing way. The business department of Haifa University has a unique philosophy for their aim is to have their students study in a homely atmosphere. In order to accomplish this, each new student on their MBA program is required to join their classmates for a full day before the beginning of school year for a time of community building at a kibbutz in the north. Students join in games prepared to forge them into community and help them get to know one other.

One of the exercises when I started school there involved all 33 students in my class being asked to imagine that a large carpet on the floor was a map of Israel. We were to stand approximately on the location of the geographical place from which we'd just come. I stood on the north side rather close to the "border" with Lebanon, exactly where I estimated that Nazareth would be. Almost everyone else came from my general area, with an exception from Tel-Aviv and another from Jerusalem.

After we finished the get-acquainted exercise, we proceeded to the next game. This time we were asked to think of the carpet as a map of the world and told to stand on the country where their paternal grandmother was born. Amazingly, there were only five Arabs in the class who stood where Palestine was supposed to be—the rest were scattered throughout Europe, North Africa, other Middle East countries, and even America. The five Arabs included two Christians, two Muslims and one Druze—all with deep indigenous roots in the land. The others were Jewish colleagues, all newcomers to Palestine/Israel. After a moment of embarrassed silence, our leader quickly moved to the next exercise.

The Law of Return states that anyone deemed to be of Jewish extraction has a right to "return" to Israel. But that right of immigration contradicts the basic principle of equality, as we experienced personally in our own family. My sister Samar's story, published in *Haaretz*, exemplifies this problem.

After Samar completed her studies at the Nazareth Baptist School she went on for higher education as a food engineer to the prestigious Technion Institute in Haifa where she earned her B.S. and then continued her studies getting a Masters degree in health administration at an extension of Clark University in Haifa. Part of her studies involved being on campus in the Boston area. After graduating she began working for Israel's Ministry of Health as a health inspector in food factories in the Galilee region, issuing certificates of approval for their facilities and manufacturing food procedures.

Samar is a committed Christian believer and during her school days she was active in the Evangelical students' ministry and was later elected as a coördinator for the Sunday school ministry in our church and, in fact, became the first ordained deaconess in our church. In 2000 at a church conference Samar met a young Jordanian named Rajai from Irbid in northern Jordan.

Rajai was an energetic minister in the Life Agape ministries of Jordan and the two shared a zeal for ministry. They began to keep in touch via e-mail and shortly thereafter, they met again to talk more seriously and finally decided to get married. As is our custom in the Middle East, Rajai came to Nazareth to ask my father's permission and in November, 2001, they were married at a lovely ceremony in the Lutheran church of Amman. They started their life together in a house Rajai had renovated in Fuhais, a small Christian town near Amman. Samar, of course, resigned from the Israeli Ministry of Health and joined her husband in his ministry and life in Amman.

In 2003 my mother got seriously ill, so the young couple who now had a baby girl called Farah [meaning "joy"] decided to move and live in Nazareth so Samar could help nurse our mother. Also, the para-church organization with which they were ministering in Jordan had just started operating in Israel and the West Bank and they needed experienced workers in Israel. However the Israeli government refused my brother-in- law's request to come live in

Nazareth. Unfortunately Rajai was Jordanian. In Israel's eyes, an Arab is an Arab and they do not care from what country he hails. To "preserve" the pure Jewish aspect of Israel, they are reluctant to bring in more Arabs to live in Israel even if their spouse is Israeli.

The fact that my sister worked in the Ministry of Health for several years carried no weight, nor that our father was a journalist in the prestigious Israeli-Hebrew newspaper *Haaretz* for 33 years, nor the fact that one of her brothers owns and manages a software company in Nazareth that conducts international business while the other directs a prominent school in Nazareth.

Our appeals to the Ministry of Interior to change their decision amicably or even through media pressure was to no avail. (Uzi Benziman from *Haaretz* wrote an article about the case and Yair Etinger from the same paper included their story in a piece he did on other similar families in an article titled "Every Arab Is a Potential Terrorist".) Nothing succeeded.

Finally we filed a lawsuit in the Supreme Court. The state's lawyer asked for several extensions from the court—which were granted—but finally several months later he capitulated and let the court know they would allow my brother-in-law a permit of entrance and enroll him in a family unification process.

This case left a bitter taste in our mouths for we experienced in our own family this overt discrimination, all the while knowing any Jew or someone remotely connected to Jewish people from any corner of the world could come to Israel at any time and immediately get a newcomer's permit with all the rights that accompany this. My sister, born here, with ancestors on this land going back for centuries, was given the choice to either be distanced from her husband or from her parents.

It is not just the laws and practices that discriminate against the Arabs in Israel but the popular anti-Arab statements of anger and outrage that are common in Israel. As Arabs in Israel we find it difficult to accept the extent freedom of expression is given to rabid, racist politicians who call for the general deportation of all Arabs from this country. For a long time and before it was outlawed, the "Kach" movement originated by the American rabbi Meir Kahane openly fomented against all Arabs demanding we all be deported and stripped of our homeland.

I remember as a student hearing this racist rabbi at a rally at the Hebrew University in Jerusalem calling us "Arab dogs" and demanding we be thrown out of the country. At that point he was pelted with rotten eggs and the police shut down the rally to protect him—but he was still granted freedom of speech and the police chased us on horses into the university dorms! Or perhaps it would be better to say he was given license to poison the minds of those who listened to his rant.

We can never accept stretching the right of expression to incorporate giving the right to such an arch-racist person like Kahane to throw mud and poison on native citizens of this country, demanding their transfer by force from their traditional homeland—without compensation for property that has belonged to their family for generations.

In 1990 while working at a law office in Jerusalem I was going from one government office to another to submit some papers when I came to Jaffa Street near the main post office via the new gate route and noticed a crowd milling around some police cars. I asked a bystander what was happening. He said, "An Arab bastard stabbed two old men at the bus stop here and ran away."

I was dressed in a lawyerly fashion, but suddenly I was afraid this stranger would figure out that I was an Arab myself. He didn't. Soon the mob began shouting "Death to Arabs." I slowly slipped away before being recognized.

Such incidents happen too frequently for comfort. One evening I was strolling with my wife in a beautiful neighborhood of Nazareth where the view across the Jezreel Valley to Mount Tabour and Mount Precipice is spectacular. Suddenly we noticed a crowd of people on the porch of one of the villas who were shouting. Getting closer we heard them screaming, accusing and cursing someone who appeared to be the owner of the house.

Suddenly we heard a woman scream, "You betrayed us. I will pursue you your entire life. How could you do such a thing to us?" Another was shouting: "You are bringing Muhammad to the neighborhood. We will be forced to hear '*Allah Akbar*' [the Muslim call of prayer].We will never forgive you for that." Apparently the owner had sold his house to an Arab and the neighbors were furious that the purity of the neighborhood was damaged.

In 2004, as part of my preparation to move from the legal world to my current job at the Nazareth Baptist School I participated in a course geared to school administrators held at a university in Israel. One of the participants, a high official in the Ministry of Education, shared with the class her theory that Bedouins are deficient genetically and this causes a vast, unbridgeable gap between them and the rest of the population! The lecturer, a knowledgeable scholar, gave her an appropriate response dismantling her "theory" that would not have shamed the Nazi regime. Instead of repenting for discriminating against the Bedouins for years, this Ministry of Education official continued to justify her prejudices.

The Bible tells us in God's sight there is neither Jew, Greek, male or female. Jesus taught the world what equality was about, and we as Christ's followers are obliged to advocate for equality among all peoples—including Jews in Israel who are not exempt from the Biblical mandate.

As Arab citizens of Israel we face ugly racism on a continual basis and we have learned to just keep turning the other cheek, walking away from such incidents to preclude causing more controversy. Besides, how do you fight such deep-rooted, anti-Arab sentiments?

Our marginalization is also accompanied with rigid treatment from officials towards us as Arabs. One such incident happened with me personally. In the summer of 1983 I had finished my matriculation exams, traveled to Denmark to a youth camp and then on to Germany to visit my aunt before coming back home. I was awaiting to see what would happen with my applications for universities, but in the meantime I planned to work and save some money. A friend of my dad spoke to the human resources director of a chocolate company in Nazareth Ilit. It was a delightful prospect to work somewhere where you could eat unlimited amounts of chocolate. Several meetings with the director were canceled, but at last a meeting was set and I went by bus to the factory. The guard at the entrance asked me the purpose of my visit and I told him that I had a meeting scheduled with the human resource director. He checked while I waited at the gate, but came back to tell me the director was not there! He apologized but said he could not let me in. I tried to convince him to change his mind to let me wait inside for the director to return, but in vain.

I left the gate frustrated and angry and began walking away. We were in the pre-cellular phone era, so I began to look around for a phone to contact the human resources office to check what had happened. Some 200 yards away I noted a small police station. Naïvely I thought that a police station was a good place to ask for help, so I went in and saw a policeman sitting behind a counter writing something. I was still upset and without any introduction just asked the policeman if I could use the phone. The policeman lifted his head and started shouting: "Who do think you are? Do you think this is a public phone here?"

I was furious and started shouting back even louder telling him he should be ashamed of himself for giving me such an answer. Immediately doors opened and some men came into the room—some in uniforms, others not. They pushed me into one of the rooms and shut the door. I remembered stories I'd read in local papers about Arab prisoners tortured by extinguishing burning cigarettes on their naked bodies. Before they had time to say anything I asserted to them in Hebrew: "If you touch me, my dad will cut you into pieces." I used an uncommon term in Hebrew for "cut you into pieces," but one I knew was pejorative.

One of the men, not in uniform, said, "Even if Begin [the Israeli prime minister] is your father that does not give you the right to come in and shout at the policeman." I answered, "But he started it." This dialogue continued and then he asked who my father was. When I told him, their tone began to calm down. He asked me to apologize for my shouting before the policeman. I tried to justify my "criminal" behavior but he insisted so I uttered half an apology. He then said: "You want to use the phone? Go ahead!"

I have often wondered what would have happened if my father was not a journalist so that touching me, even slightly, would bring them aggravation?

One place where our Israeli identity is tested most tangibly is at the Ben Gurion airport on our way in or out of the country. Every Arab who has traveled abroad can regale you with stories of harassment by the Israeli security. We are not unaware of the need for tight security because of the history of what has happened there, but the interrogation and the searching of luggage can be done respectfully. We have traveled in enough foreign countries to know there is sophisticated equipment available to screen luggage and identify suspected items, but these are not used in Israel with Arabs. It appears they prefer to use harsher measures, with endless, almost silly questions, making traveling abroad almost to be dreaded.

In 1999 I went to the U.S. to attend a convocation for lawyers in Washington D.C. At Ben Gurion airport when my turn came to go through security, since they knew I was Arab, someone was assigned to accompany me through the terminal and escort me to a small room for special screening. There I found another Arab in a colorful shirt with the contents of his king-sized bag spread all over the counter being checked by two security women with nylon gloves who were treating him as if he were a drug smuggler.

It seemed like undue harassment and humiliation, so I began speaking to him in Arabic. Originally he had come from a small village near Nablus in the West Bank, but he had lived in the U.S. for ten years and was traveling back to the U.S. after his first visit to his home village since emigrating. His old mother had packed him with different seeds and traditional spices and foods so her son would get proper healthy nutrition in the land of hamburgers and French fries. To annoy the security officers we spoke and laughed in Arabic about different issues until they completed my check (including a body check!).

Sometimes these officials are surprised, as they appeared to be a couple of years ago when a friend of mine came to Israel for a visit. Here is his story: "I had the honor of being part of a group of people from Nazareth and abroad (mainly America and Britain) who coöperated in establishing a village in the fashion of Nazareth in the time of Jesus called 'Nazareth Village.' President Jimmy Carter and his wife Rosalyn were appointed presidents emeriti for the project and on one of his visits to Nazareth, an American colleague brought a framed letter of support and endorsement from the presidential couple to be hung at the entrance of this 'living museum' of Nazareth Village and to encourage support of the place.

"The Israeli security guard knew our friend would be staying in Arab Nazareth so asked him the standard questions about carrying any present or anything someone had given him to bring it to Israel. Remembering the letter our friend said, 'Actually, I do.' She asked to see the item, so he pulled the framed letter from the Carters out of his luggage and handed it to her. She looked closely with shocked eyes and then took the letter hastily (but carefully) to her supervisor. The news spread among the security personnel and in a few minutes most of them were gathered around the letter and our amused friend. After a few minutes, a senior official thanked our friend politely for his patience and let him go with all due respect."

In 2002 at the end of a tour in Prague a bag containing my wife's and my passports was stolen. We went through the regular process of reporting this to the Israeli consulate in Prague and a transition certificate was issued for the purpose of our return to the country. On arriving home we filed a request for a new passport and were issued temporary passports valid for a year after which we received our new permanent passports. On this document I traveled to Jordan, Egypt and the U.S. In September 2005 I flew to Britain, landing at Heathrow where I was to connect to a flight to Scotland.

When I got to "Immigration" a clerk attended me, entering my details on her computer. Then she stopped and apologizing took my passport to a different office. A few minutes later she returned and to ask about previous visits to England. I told her I'd been there three times: in 1971 as a child, in 1992 passing through Gatwick airport with my wife on our honeymoon and in 2000 through Edinburgh airport for a board meeting for Nazareth Village. She noted my answers, but kept asking more questions. After 15 minutes, the picture became clear: It seemed my passport stolen in Prague had been used by someone from the Ukraine in December 2003 trying to enter Britain, but apparently the British authorities refused his entry suspecting the passport was not his.

So I had to convince her that it was really mine, and showed her various documents to validate that fact. She kept disappearing to a back office, but then told me I would need to get a permission to let me enter from another office which would take three days. Before I could say anything she added that despite this they would permit me to enter due to "who I am." However she warned me the computer would announce this every time I tried to enter England so I should get this cleared up.

What amazed me was that this process took less than a half hour (although I felt it was longer) with no supervisor or other security officer involved. On my flight to Aberdeen I couldn't help contemplate what would have happened should an Arab be in the same situation trying to enter Israel. Would there have been a national security alert and intelligence officers involved in the interrogation? My first suspicion is that they would have first knocked the guy down and put cuffs on his hands and then, afterwards, begin to ask questions.

Many other Jewish customs are contrary to our Arab culture here in Israel. As an Arab-Christian lawyer my day off was on Sunday and generally the judicial system here takes that into consideration. In the Nazareth area, there are many Christian lawyers who do not work on Sundays so generally Sunday hearings are not set. If this does happen, usually a standard request for change of date is enough to reschedule to another day, but there are exceptions.

Once I had a case before a Jewish woman judge that needed to be postponed. The judge wanted to set the next date on a Sunday, but I reminded her as a Christian I do not work on Sundays. She impatiently said that was the only date available. Despite my protests she scheduled the case on a Sunday and I told her I would file a written request for a date change. When I returned to my office, I was seething at what I perceived to be her insensitive response. I whimsically considered making her really angry by suggesting a Saturday session. Just then I found a fax from the judge setting us a non-Sunday hearing.

There are ways to irritate the "other" and ways to accommodate differences. Both the Jews and the Arabs in Israel need to learn tolerance towards one another's culture. We must continue to challenge Israeli laws that discriminate against Christian practices, but we need to maintain respect for one another if we are to forge a community where differences are allowed and appreciated.

It is not just marginalization and stiff behavior but also inequality in an institutional manner. When I was a child my father had a journalist friend who used to visit us with his family of two sons. He was an American Jew who worked for a foreign press and the boys were roughly the ages of my brother and me, so we became good friends. When they visited us in Nazareth we took them to the open-area playground on a nearby hillside where we had a soccer field delineated with barrels and stones. When we visited them in Tel-Aviv, they would take us to their country club with soccer fields, tennis courts and an Olympic-sized swimming pool. At the time, Nazareth with 50,000 inhabitants did not even have a swimming pool.

The obvious gaps between Arab lifestyle in our towns and villages compared to what is available in Jewish communities can only be attributed to intentional inequality. We see this in Nazareth and Nazareth Illit (a new Jewish town established on lands confiscated from neighboring Arab villages 50 years ago). Nazareth remains a neglected old town with endless traffic jams, while the Jewish community has an infrastructure similar to a modern town in Europe or North America—yet Arabs and Jews pay the same taxes.

True, the economic situation of Arabs in Israel on average is better than in most Arab countries, but this is no excuse for preferential treatment given to the Jewish communities. This planned marginalization of the Arabs in Israel produces a lack of respect for the law, and Arabs subsequently have a higher crime rate ranging from minor traffic tickets to the most serious offenses. Since Arabs do not identify themselves with the country, they find it easier to disregard the laws of the land.

Respect for the rule of law is difficult when the Arab population feels discriminated against. Repeatedly one hears or experiences situations that demonstrate that in Israel there is a two-tiered culture and unless you're Jewish or have access to people in power, you will constantly be discriminated against—whether you're Arab or European or from a Third World country. What is necessary is to learn that you have to be prepared for the persecution and stand up to the bullies. As Teddy Roosevelt said, you need to learn to speak softly, but at the same time manage to carry a big stick.

12

Braking Christian Emigration

As noted, returning from their captivity in Babylon, those faithful workers who labored to rebuild the walls of Jerusalem needed something more than building material, for they had to protect themselves (and the work itself) by carrying a sword in the other hand. The sword is a prominent weapon in ancient Arab culture and there are 300 names for "sword" in Arabic. Ancient poems are replete with the symbol of a sword. On the other hand, the Bible talks about the sword of the Spirit (Eph 6:17): the Word of God—used to protect and defend the believers.

Living in a hostile environment requires using symbolic bricks to build the community and something as effective as swords to defend the building process. So just like Nehemiah's workers who held a sword in one hand, while building with the other, we are asked to hold a sword too—not one for killing but one for defending us in the spiritual sphere: *For we wrestle not against flesh and blood, but against principalities, against powers, against the rulers of the darkness of this world, against spiritual wickedness in high places* (Eph 6:12).

Furthermore, where the world tries to conform the Christian and the church into its own mold, our spiritual swords serve to protect from that: *"And be not conformed to this world: but be ye transformed by the renewing of your mind, that ye may prove what is that good, and acceptable, and perfect, will of God"* (Rom 12:2).

One huge battle we Arab Christians face is the constant struggle against emigrating out of the Holy Land. There's a comic folk Arab song from the days of the British Mandate where the singer addresses the British high commissioner, "OHHHH commissioner, tell your country that London has become the stable of our horses."

Unfortunately, after the days of the British Mandate, the easiest way to cope with the hostilities and racism visited on the Arab-Christian community was to emigrate, so today Detroit and Lansing, Michigan; Los Angeles; Sydney, Australia; Toronto and even New York have become the new Meccas for the Christian-Arab community of the Middle East. Tens of thousands have emigrated in the last half-century, finding peace and rest in a foreign land.

America especially has become a refuge for Arab Christians in the Middle East. Generally it is easier for Arab Christians in Israel to emigrate than it is for Palestinian Christians from the West Bank or for Iraqi- and Lebanese-Christians. Also, as a scorned minority group in the Holy Land, Arab-Christians have been coerced into leaving their homeland in search of security and a place to earn a living wage.

On the one hand, the Christians in Israel suffer discrimination from the harsh practices of the Israeli state against all Arabs; on the other hand the majority Muslim population doesn't include them in their circles because of religious differences. Israel claims to be a democratic state, but their concept of citizenship does not extend to the non-Jewish population. Philosophically the state of Israel is required to deal with its Arab citizens from all denominations and religions equally, for they are all Israeli citizens. In actuality their practices are at odds with their philosophy.

Often the entire Arab population is grouped together with violent Muslim and Druze groups in the Arab community, so many Christian-Arabs reluctantly arrive at the conclusion that it is preferable to quit and leave their homeland in order to seek their fortune elsewhere than try to cope with the unreasonable requirements placed on the Arab population. There is also the prejudicial treatment that comes from Muslims or Druze who often violate their neighboring Christian community residents while the Israeli police stand aside idly watching these attacks.

In 1981 the Druze began a pogrom against Christian houses in the village of Kufur Yassif because a Druze youngster had been stabbed by an Arab-Christian youth during a fight at a soccer match. At the time we went to the village to see the results of the hostilities there because my father had a friend in the village whom he wanted to visit during the difficulties. As a journalist my father was able to report on this clash that had happened and the story was published in the Jewish newspaper *Haaretz*.

Seeing blood on the ground at the entrance to the house of a Christian policeman who was killed in the attack was a most sobering experience. My wife originated from that village and the scar of this barbaric attack has never really healed for those villagers who are still traumatized by what happened.

Another Druze mob attacked Arab-Christians in February, 2005, in the village of Mughar, just 20 miles northeast of Nazareth. Fortunately the Christians were able to flee for their lives and miraculously there were no casualties, even though much damage was done to their property in their absence. The cause of the hostility turned out to be based on a false rumor that blamed an Arab-Christian lad for something that a Druze boy had actually done.

The Druze also are a maligned and persecuted people, because the Israelis have used them to implement their dirty police tactics in the West Bank. In order to prove their loyalty to their Israeli counterparts, Druze who serve in the army are at times crueler to the Palestinians than the Jewish soldiers. After serving three years in the military, they return to their village not knowing who they are. Both the Muslims and Christians treat them as pariahs for having joined the enemy army just to earn money and have access to schooling. But no one in the village is willing to hire them, so they join Druze gangs and become village outcasts.

These dynamics produce a tinderbox, ready to explode at the slightest provocation. Once I took an American reporter after a Druze-Christian confrontation to the village of Mughar where we encountered a young women, originally from there but who was married living nearby in the village of Rama. She came to rescue her parents from the fighting and was standing forlornly by a van that held her parents' most precious belongings. Never will I forget the anguish on her face as she prepared to take them with her back to Rama, even though she knew that a couple of years before in Rama a Druze mob had attacked Christians fiercely and they continued to harass Christians. With tears running down her face, she admitted it wasn't that much safer in Rama, but at least they would be together. No wonder it seems obvious to any outside observer that anyone in the country who could move away would try to leave the Holy Land.

During such clashes, the police and the law enforcement authorities do little to scale-back the violence. Their silence and inactivity borders on criminal negligence, but it appears incidents of Muslim mob violence against Arab-Christian houses are ignored by the law enforcement agencies because orders have come down from the Israeli government officials that they should exploit any disputes between Muslims and Christians in order to foment trouble between them and get them all to leave the country.

What can you do in such cases? We offered prayers for those hurt and with our limited means informed our friends worldwide that their support and awareness were essential, just as the Christian presence in the Middle East is of great importance. This can be manifested through letters to the Israeli government asking them to perform their duties with equal law enforcement or also by strengthening relationships with Christians abroad.

My father grew up in a culture that maintained a sensitive balance between Christians, Jews and Muslims through mutual respect and tolerance. After years of peaceful coexistence, this threshold was breached and peace was lost and now ugly scars around us remind us that we live in perilous times.

The Christian minority in Israel is educated, works hard, loves life, preserves the law of the country and is not violent. The influence of the compassionate, loving, forgiving teaching of Jesus Christ has softened the hearts of the Christian community, including even those who are not affiliated closely with the church or with faith.

Yet Israel continues to discriminate against its Christian citizens and it has been proven in many instances that the law does not protect all citizens equally. Emigration to the West is encouraged and the Christian presence is steadily diminishing so the fear is that the Holy Land will be emptied of its followers of the Holy One and turned into a kind of religious theme park where visitors can see the sights, but where Christians are not welcomed to stay.

Remaining a Christian presence in this land of conflict and violence is not easy. As the situation becomes more difficult economically, socially and politically, holding on to an indigenous Christian presence here becomes harder, especially for those who are weary of the strikes and counter-strikes of those people who prefer to maintain a violent conflict and dispute over the land. Also, emigration is much easier for those fluent in English with relatives who live abroad.

At one point I declared I would be the last to turn off the lights when all the Christians had left the country. Today I am more jaded and feel that loving the land where our Lord was raised is not enough—I must work for a transformative change for the better in the land of our Lord and Savior Jesus Christ. This purpose gives me the power to continue and believe even when there seems to be continual war all around, and the prospect of peace in our times seems remote.

So we strive to keep Christians living in the Middle East as part of the remarkable mosaic of people here who have made priceless contributions to its development. Their continued presence here is proof that the inhabitants of this land are truly an enlightened people.

13

The Holocaust: Unpopular Sympathy with the Suffering of Others

The founders of Zionism wanted to establish a national home for the Jews who had suffered around the world from persecution and anti-Jewish activities which peaked with the Holocaust in World War II. This dreadful deed was the underpinning for the establishment of the state of Israel. The Nazi's atrocious act was not only unique in human history, but it also was accompanied by virtual silence from the rest of the civilized world.

No words can adequately describe the condemnation and disgust every person should feel towards such awful Satanic activities. I am thus shocked when a Jewish public servant in Israel calls an opponent or even an enemy by such a description. Maybe that person should be punished by sending them to Yad Vashem (the Holocaust Museum in Jerusalem) so such slanderers can understand the absurdity of such words. It also exasperates me when any Arab denies the Holocaust's happening or the number of causalities it caused.

As people who are slated to live together in this country and for the sake of our development as a healthy, moral and mature society, we should recognize the suffering of the other without asking for any special recognition. We are not talking about merchandise or negotiations, but rather about an important moral position.

Talking about the Holocaust raises a range of reactions in the Arab world that go from resentment to discomfort. The annual siren for the memory of the Holocaust causalities (like the beep for the memory of the causalities of Israeli soldiers and the standing for the national anthem) becomes an embarrassing rite for every Arab in Israel.

I was with a client in a lawyer's office in Tel-Aviv involved in a long and tiring negotiation, attempting to settle a case my client had with the company the other lawyer represented. The negotiations went on and it became dark. The others in the law firm went home leaving the three of us behind. Suddenly the siren for the victims of the Holocaust blew. The situation was embarrassing but in order to be sensitive to my colleague, all of us stood around the table. In those moments, my prayers and thoughts wandered.

According to Hitler's lists, Arabs were next on the list for the final solution, so just from a practical point of view, Arabs should be the first to identify with the atrocities the Jews suffered from his bloody hands. As part of the human race, Arabs should have protested with all civilized nations calling that an awful act that should never be allowed to happen again. However, Arabs are an emotional people who have suffered much at the hands of Israel, and they find it difficult to differentiate between condemnation of the Holocaust and sympathy with its casualties and condemnation of Israel's policies and deeds today.

Adding to this confusion is what appears today to be irrational and unconditional support and sympathy for the Jews stemming from feelings of collective guilt in countries like Germany, Holland and the U.S. Unfortunately these guilt feelings are manipulated and used by Israel for materialistic benefit or political support. We in Israel often observe how ranking international guests are welcomed with ceremonies that always highlight the Holocaust in an effort to blackmail sympathy and support for Israel's actions today that have nothing to do with the atrocities of the Nazis 65 years ago.

Often international guests are driven directly from the Ben Gurion airport to the Holocaust Museum in Jerusalem and then given a helicopter tour above Israel so they can see how narrow the country of Israel actually is and the short distance between the West Bank villages and the settlements in Israel. To us who live here this appears to be nothing more than Israeli manipulation of guests to make them feel guilty about the world's silence regarding the Holocaust and then emphasizing how geographically vulnerable Israel is to the dangers of living cheek-and-jowl with Arab settlements, so all their hostile behavior is necessary to preclude another holocaust happening.

Current advanced technology and long-range missiles have proven this argument of the dangers of geographical proximity is moot. Cities over 80 kilometers south of the Lebanese border shelled in the second Lebanese war in 2006 proved that point. Peace happens in the hearts and through trust—no barriers can stand before hatred and its attempt to cause damage.

Most Arabs regard the Western support of Israel as proof of the world's hypocrisy—especially since the problem of Palestinian refugees as well as the Palestinian homeland (approved for solution in several UN decisions) is still unresolved. Furthermore, many Arabs identify with the Jewish Holocaust victims whose suffering produced the Zionist movement that decided they should have a homeland of their own in Palestine— at the expense of the Arab Palestinians (without even considering the issue that these Palestinians did nothing to contribute to that happening). No wonder Arabs feel that the Palestinians are left to pay a heavy price for a Holocaust they had no part in producing.

Arabs and others also protest what is seen as a claim for monopoly on the pain Jews have suffered as result of the Holocaust. But it always depends on whose ox is being gored. Everyone tends to see their own troubles as the heaviest and most unique in the world—but this is merely an egocentric view that discounts their neighbors' pain.

Some three decades ago my father was involved in publishing the first private local Arabic weekly newspaper called *Assenara*. Two retired teachers decided to publish a competing newspaper calling it *Venus* and one of their first editorials called the Palestinian people the "Jesus of the 20th century," illustrating this with a picture of Palestinians superimposed on the image of Jesus on the cross. I reacted negatively to this and wrote a letter to the editor explaining that Palestinians are not the only ones to suffer in the 20th century and we should recall the holocaust of the Armenians and the holocaust of the Jews which were far more horrific and also that no suffering of a people can be equated to the suffering of a sinless Jesus Christ who died on the cross to redeem the whole human race from their sin.

The editors published my letter with a lengthy comment and mean-spirited rebuttal that claimed I was insensitive to Arab suffering, but I remain steadfast in my conclusions that no "patriot" can equate the suffering of their own people to that of our Savior and fortunately those I regarded highly commended me for my courage in taking a stand for Christ.

My beloved Christian education teacher, the late George Laty, who had invited me to play football and attend the revival evangelistic meetings in church where I took my first decision for Christ, saw me after this was published and commended me on the courage of taking a stand for Christ. That meant a lot to me from my old teacher who was struggling with illness at that point.

My father recommended I wait a few days and then go speak to the editors personally. This worked and I convinced them I had not meant to disregard Palestinian suffering altogether, so they published a clarification to pacify the situation and called me a "polite young man" that contrary to their first impression obviously did love the Palestinian people.

However, in the eyes of many Arabs, the suffering of the Palestinians is the greatest on earth. They feel this deeply and this precludes their being able to sympathize with the Jews and their memories of the Holocaust. They also note that the Jews disregard the 20th century genocide of the Armenian people because Israel won't address this issue due to its special relationship to Turkey which was responsible for that brutal massacre.

Even hinting at the mention of the Holocaust raises hackles among the Arabs. The constant memorialization all around Israel of this event—which happened over a half century ago— while there is no effort to find a solution to the conflict with the displaced and marginalized Palestinians, make many feel the Holocaust is lifted up only as an excuse to gain sympathy for inexcusable behavior.

Painting all Arab Palestinians as inhuman, brutal and insensitive is merely evading the reality of treating them with cruelty, hostility and ruthlessness.

14

An Ending Word

A powerful Scripture that poses a challenge in this country —divided and wounded with conflict—is found in Ephesians 2:14-16.

For he himself is our peace, who has made the two one and has destroyed the barrier, the dividing wall of hostility, by abolishing in his flesh the law with its commandments and regulations. His purpose was to create in himself one new man out of the two, thus making peace, and in this one body to reconcile both of them to God through the cross, by which he put to death their hostility.

How can the body of Christ consisting of Arab Evangelicals like myself, Messianic Jews and expatriates be one when the peoples that we belong to are in conflict?

A friend of mine uses the following symbolic picture to identify the solution: Only the big brother Jesus can reconcile Jacob and Esau. Jacob is Israel and the father of the twelve tribes. He has the promises. Esau is the spiritual descendant of Hagar the Arab. Only the Prince of Peace can tear down the separation wall and the heavy layers of thousands of years of prejudice and hatred.

This reconciliation process is a slow one and needs a lot of work. Love that is reflected in warmth is capable of bringing a change in attitude. Palestinians have developed a conspiracy mentality because for decades they have trusted various leaders to help them regain their rights—all in vain. Their hopes have been dashed. Now the jaundiced view of the Palestinians is to attribute any goodwill gesture or position to a hidden agenda.

Israel, too, assumes a wary stance—especially as a result of past experiences like the Holocaust. It also needs love and warmth in order to heal the persecution complexes which persist. Two leaders have excellently filled the role of a loving and skillful, yet gentle, friend—President Bill Clinton and King Hussein from Jordan.

The first became the most beloved personality among the Israeli people, reflecting warmth and appreciation to the entire populace of Israel. This gracious president with his Southern accent knew how to shake hands and how to push the right buttons. From his gentle talk about peace, to his quoting the Hebrew prophets and his skilled, spontaneous playing of a saxophone, he captivated the populace with his penetrating eyes and fatherly stance. His remarkable memorial speech for his friend Yitzhak Rabin will long be remembered as will the Hebrew term he invented and made popular "Shalom Haver," meaning "shalom my friend."

The gracious king from Jordan also had an almost magical effect on the country. But King Hussein brought more than just his gentle and fatherly talk—he added his deep wisdom and cultural understanding—all expressed in proper Arabic and British English which endeared him to all those saw him—and few will ever forget his kneeling down compassionately and humbly near the wailing woman in biet Shemesh after the attack in Aram Nahariem by a Jordanian soldier.

These two leaders have shown authentic love to the Israeli people. They were not flattering and this was appreciated by the people and the leaders who have had to overcome their paranoid complexes from their horrific history. Unfortunately, no high profile Christian leader or ministry has been effective in bringing reconciliation in this troubled region.

We would have expected that those who follow the Prince of Peace and the One who brought reconciliation between heaven and earth would be capable of playing a role in reconciliation between

Arabs and Jews in the same land that the Lord lived in—"the Holy Land."

I have tried to play a role in a limited way to help bring more understanding between conflicting parties. A few years ago, I joined the advisory board of *Musalaha* ["reconciliation" in Arabic] whose aims are to bring various parts of the body of the Messiah to live together peaceably with understanding and openness towards one another. This organization is not only performing a vital task in reconciliation activities between Arabs and Jewish followers of Christ but recently also between Muslims and Christians.

I firmly believe that both Arabs and Jews have been destined to live together in this country; therefore programs for reconciliation and dialogue are important. These tenets we have been promoting in our school through various joint activities with Jewish schools in areas such as music, computer courses and even a circus program! Out of these experiences, we have formed a forum for education in Israel that includes all Arab Evangelical and Messianic Jewish educational institutions whose aim is to bring mutual enrichment for the glory of God through faith-based education.

As an Arab Palestinian Evangelical Christian living in Nazareth, Israel, I constantly struggle trying to rebuild the wall with bricks in one hand, maintaining a sword in the other to serve Jesus in his own hometown. In other cases we struggle to be salt or light and always to be witnesses for the Lord.

My efforts in this book were to share some of the points of friction and contradictions of our lives here in order to help my soul be reconciled to our mission here in Nazareth. With God's grace we will continue to serve the Lord with gladness and with the tools given to us in this special and unique location of Nazareth. The people of Nazareth were angry with Jesus in the synagogue when he mentioned two Gentile figures as heroes of faith after reading them the passage from Isaiah (Lk 4). They wanted to throw him from the mountain that their town was built upon. Jesus just passed through the crowd and Nazareth rejected him then.

In all due humility, we simple servants are trying to bring the glory of Jesus back to his hometown where he was rejected.

Nazareth Village scene

With Abir and kids in
Nativity church

On the left with brother and
friends in Eynsham, England

With grandfathers 1967

In Nazareth Baptist
school yard (on the left)
with dad, brother and
sister 1976